*One Minute Service®* — these three words in the title offer a glimpse into what is truly a wide and rather underutilized variety of topics of servicing customers. Well-organized and easy to understand, this book captures first impressions, quick issue resolutions, and everything in between. You and your team will discover practical service keys for satisfying your customers. The keys themselves aren't revolutionary, but applying them might just provide the revolution your company needs.

—NICK ANTON
Human Resources Specialist, Nissan Corporation

The market has long clamored for a simple, concise guide to great customer service geared to frontline employees. *One Minute Service®* is it! Bruce Loeffler has provided every business manager with an invaluable tool that can train employees to provide great service for every customer. Wise leaders will stock this book by the dozens and make it mandatory reading for every employee.

—BILLY RIGGS
Author and Motivational Speaker

# One Minute SERVICE®

## Keys to Providing Great Service
## Like Disney World

### Bruce Loeffler

## DC
### PRESS

A Division of the Diogenes Consortium

SANFORD • FLORIDA

Published by DC Press
2445 River Tree Circle
Sanford, FL 32771
http://www.focusonethics.com

For orders other than individual consumers, DC Press grants discounts on purchases of 10 or more copies of single titles for bulk use, special markets, or premium use. For further details, contact:
Special Sales — DC Press
2445 River Tree Circle, Sanford, FL 32771
TEL: 866-602-1476

Book set in: Adobe Jenson Pro
Cover Design and Composition: Jonathan Pennell

**Library of Congress Cataloging-in-Publication Data**
Loeffler. Bruce
One Minute Service: Keys to Providing Great Service Like Disney World
ISBN: 978-1-932021-44-8

First DC Press Edition
10  9  8  7  6  5  4  3  2  1
Printed and bound in the United States of America. Printed on acid-free paper.

*One Minute Service® is dedicated to the memory of my parents,*

*Lowell and Wilma Loeffler, who are now celebrating in Heaven;*

*I miss them, I miss their counsel, and I am eternally grateful*

*for the foundation and encouragement they have given me.*

# CONTENTS

**Chapter 1. Attitude *Makes* the Difference** .............. 1

   A.  Attitude Is a Choice ............................6

   B.  Keep It Positive .................................. 16

   C.  Be Your Best ........................................ 18

**Chapter 2. G — the Greet Key** ............................ 23

   A.  Welcome Them.................................... 28

   B.  Initiate the Interaction....................... 30

   C.  Phone Sets the Tone .......................... 34

**Chapter 3. R — the Relate Key** ........................... 41

   A.  Connect with Them ........................... 45

   B.  Build a Relationship........................... 48

   C.  Personalize Your Service .................... 52

**Chapter 4. E — the Exceed Key** .......................... 59

   A.  Apply the Power of Asking................. 66

   B.  Be Exceptional ..................................... 69

   C.  Go the Extra Mile............................... 73

**Chapter 5. A — the Affirm Key** ......................... 81

   A.  Validate Each Person.......................... 83

   B.  Invest in Others.................................. 86

   C.  Recovery Is Essential........................... 90

**Chapter 6. T — the Thank Key**............................**95**

  A.  Thank Your Customers ....................................98

  B.  Find Other Ways to Say Thank You............102

  C.  Thank Your Co-workers and Your Boss......105

**Chapter 7. The Likeability Factor** ......................**113**

  A.  Be Friendly ......................................................115

  B.  Be Courteous....................................................120

  C.  Get Along..........................................................123

**Concluding Thoughts**...........................................**131**

**End Notes** .............................................................**135**

# FOREWORD

I FIRST MET BRUCE IN 1989 when he worked for Walt Disney World. Bruce was kind enough to give me a behind-the-scenes tour of a company whose name has become synonymous with excellent service. Like so many, you have probably been to a Disney property too and been awed by their excellent, friendly service and wondered, "How do they do that?" Well, look no further. The essence of the Disney methods for creating an outstanding service culture is spelled out in *One Minute Service*® by someone who spent years living and working in it. Better yet, Bruce has come up with his own unique formula for teaching and applying the techniques in less than a minute.

Bruce's hands-on experience at Disney is invaluable. His personality, education, and other experience in the business world make him uniquely qualified to write a great book about how to provide excellent customer service — and he has. As I read the manuscript I kept nodding in agreement with so many of the concepts he presents: first impressions are critical; little things make a big difference; attitude and likeability are vital attributes; and recovering from service mistakes quickly is essential.

If you are looking for ways to provide excellent, frontline customer service, this is it. This book will teach you and your team members the keys to outstanding service in a simple, easy-to-understand, no-nonsense fashion. Better yet, the title *One Minute Service*® is not an empty promise. It's the essence of what makes this book so special. Although this is a short book, please don't be deceived by its brevity. It's loaded with action-ready, immediately applicable ideas for providing great customer service and almost all of them can be achieved in just a few seconds.

We live in a world where businesses are endlessly obsessed with numbers and the bottom line. Yet those numbers are driven by the behaviors of customers and the people who serve them. Any business that pays attention to the numbers at the expense of ignoring customers places itself in serious jeopardy. All successful organizations revolve around the care and feeding of customers.

I urge you to read this book, reflect on its wisdom, and share it with your team members. The result will be a more enjoyable workplace for customers and for everyone in your organization — and a more profitable one too.

—**Michael LeBoeuf**
Author of *How to Win Customers and Keep Them for Life*

# INTRODUCTION

WOULD YOU AGREE that we live in a fast-paced society? Customers want everything right now. They want fast food, instant potatoes, jiffy this, quick that, drive-through service, instant messaging, and in-and-out burgers and they aren't willing to wait. I call it a microwave mentality and when we don't deliver Excellence in an Instant©, they aren't happy. *One Minute Service* is dedicated to providing excellent service to your customers in an instant.

Over the past forty years, America has moved from a goods and services economy to primarily a service economy. In many cases, service has become *the product*. If you want your company to grow, then you must understand that service often is *the experience*.

Today's customers are looking for three basics: good value, consistent quality, and excellent service. Yet, they are becoming increasingly dissatisfied with the poor service or lack of service they encounter in virtually every business and industry. As a result, businesses are losing customers in droves.

Research attributed to TARP, the Technical Assistance Research Program, posed an interesting question: Why do customers leave your business and go to your competitor? Here are the primary reasons given: 1% die, 3% move away, 5% have a friend in the business, 9% are dissatisfied with your product, and 14% are not happy with your service. The remaining 68% of customers stop doing business with your company due to just one thing: apathy on the part of your company or the employees. The reason why two-thirds of customers stop doing business with your company is because they perceive that you really don't care!

Every year corporations spend millions of dollars on what they think will improve service, yet these efforts don't work, except in select companies. The good news is that there are a few companies who still provide good, old-fashioned service. One of the companies known for excellent service is Walt Disney World.

When I lived in California, a friend of mine suggested that I audition for Disneyland's "Kids of the Kingdom," a group of ten live performers. They auditioned 300 and I was one of the fortunate ones selected. A year later Walt Disney World asked me to fulfill a three-month contract and I ended up working for Disney World for over ten years. My travels with Disney took me all across America and to Japan, England, Scandinavia, and Canada. In addition to being a professional performer in charge of several groups, I was given a unique opportunity to create my own job: to develop *Showmanship Service* for Epcot and the Magic Kingdom. I was then asked to be a supervisor in the Magic Kingdom and also spent a year in the Casting Department before moving to Texas to pursue a master's degree.

There is a lot to see and do at Disney World. I've discovered that many guests who visit Disney World have high expectations and want a great experience, good food, excellent entertainment, and quality merchandise. They also want service very quickly so they can move on to their next experience. I learned that Disney cast members needed to be efficient and effective in addition to being excellent. I soon came to the conclusion that what guests really wanted from Disney cast members, and from your organization as well, was to receive what I now call *One Minute Service*.

Disney World isn't just a theme park, *it's an experience.* Not only is it an experience for the guests, but it's also about the positive working experience Disney provides for cast members. I've discovered that how you treat your co-workers is how they in turn will treat their customers. So, in reality, your first customer is not the public, but rather each of your co-workers who in turn serve guests and each other.

Walt Disney World is different from other companies in numerous ways, but none more distinct than Disney terminology. You see, Disney doesn't have customers; they have *guests.* They don't have employees; they have *cast members.*

You aren't hired for a job; you're cast into a *role*; and in that role, you work either *onstage* (around the guests) or *backstage* (away from the guests). I've even noticed that other companies, such as Chick-Fil-A and Target, have begun using the term guest to refer to their customers as well.

There is no *magic formula* for why Disney is so effective. But from my experience, it is successful because Disney creates a model and an image of what excellence should look like; establishes high standards for Disney cast members to aspire to; and then trains each cast member to achieve those expectations.

Working at Disney World has provided me with some tremendous insights into service and excellence. I had the good fortune to learn from several excellent teachers and mentors. I believe that most new employees need a mentor or someone who is able to teach them the fundamentals of the job and the company. For new employees, the time spent with a mentor can literally make the difference between success and failure on the job. For me, that person was Spencer Craig.

Spencer joined Disney World in 1971 when the park opened and was a manager in Merchandise, Human Resources, and the Disney University. Spencer took me "under his wing" and taught me about people, attitudes, and the Disney way of excellence. Just about everyone called Spencer "Mr. Inspiration" because he was gifted at motivating and inspiring cast members. He was superb at challenging people and developing Disney cast members to become their best. Spencer developed and taught a variety of courses, but the one that impacted me most was a motivational course called, "Wish Upon a Star." He was a great mentor and has become a life-long friend. I still bounce many of my ideas off Spencer.

As I began formulating the concepts for this book, I tried to analyze exactly what I had learned from Disney, how it has shaped the training and public speaking that I do, and why it was so effective. I wanted to define expectations from the guest's perspective and I have arrived at what I call The Five Expectations of Disney Service©. Although these expectations are not taught as such at Disney World, I believe they are the five basic ingredients that most guests want when they visit Walt Disney World — and when they visit your business as well:

### The Five Expectations of Disney Service©

+ **Excellence:** Guests want quality along with value. They want to know the company strives for excellence and its employees are providing their best effort.

+ **Experience:** Guests want their visit to be enjoyable and fun. They want to be treated as someone special and to leave with a positive experience.

- **Expediency:** Guests want knowledgeable employees who are efficient and are able to facilitate their needs with ease and in a timely manner.

- **Enthusiasm:** Guests want employees who are outgoing, friendly, personable, and courteous and who truly enjoy helping others.

- **Empathy:** Guests want employees who can respect and relate to them and will take ownership to resolve problems quickly when they occur.

These five expectations are the real foundation of this book.

The title, *One Minute Service*®, is simply an outflow of the experiences I had at Disney World and how they can be applied to the service industry. The ideas and principles in *One Minute Service* can be applied to just about any service-related business.

# OVERVIEW

O NE MINUTE SERVICE is comprised of seven chapters. Chapters 1 and 7, on attitude and likeability, are the foundation to providing great customer service in any business. These chapters ultimately apply to every aspect of life, not just to the work you do. The keys of *One Minute Service* are found in Chapters 2 through 6 where the five elements of GREAT Service© are introduced. You see, GREAT Service isn't all that difficult! Simply stated, it is how well you understand and treat other people. The benefits of GREAT Service are that you'll become a more effective person and your company will become more successful as well.

Each chapter incorporates three specific points that define the chapter. Within those points you will find 77 ideas and tips that I learned during my years with Disney World and subsequently developed after leaving Disney. These tips are essential to the success of GREAT Service and I believe you will find them to be beneficial in your work and personal life as well.

*One Minute Service* is not designed to answer every customer service question that arises, but it is written for employees who want to gain a clearer understanding of what constitutes good service in a customer's eyes and to fine-tune their service skills. The five essential keys to GREAT Service are:

- **G**reet them: acknowledge every customer and make them feel welcome

- **R**elate to them: connect with customers and create a rapport with them

- **E**xceed their expectations: differentiate yourself from the competition

- **A**ffirm them: reinforce the importance and value of each customer

- **T**hank them: for choosing your business and encourage them to return

*It takes only a minute to be excellent.*

*One Minute Service* is designed to provide simple ideas and tools for every employee to use anytime he or she serves the customer. The tips and ideas can be used to provide excellent service in a short amount of time. When applied efficiently, all five keys can be achieved in under a minute. The beauty of each key is that you can implement one or more of the tips from each of the chapters and apply them as needed. Simply utilize the ideas that apply to your situation.

To say that working at Disney World was a positive experience would be an understatement! I learned some tremendous principles about working with others, creating excellence, and how to challenge and stretch myself and others to reach their potential. My hope is that you will see the application of *One Minute Service* in everything you do.

# ACKNOWLEDGMENTS

THANKS TO MY WONDERFUL wife Lorrie, and my two great kids, Danielle and David, for their undying patience and for letting me keep our kitchen table and piano cluttered with various chapters in progress.

Thanks to my good friend Billy Riggs for his constant prodding and the challenge of "a page a day." I would not have finished this book without your encouragement.

Thanks to Michael LeBoeuf for his help and practical ideas. Your insights were invaluable.

Thanks to Nick Anton for helping me to make sense out of this book when I was at my wits end. You gave me some well-directed insight.

Thanks to Anne Loeffler for your ideas and encouragement.

Thanks to Carolyn Lea for her editing. You have been a gem.

Most of all, thanks to my Lord and Savior, Jesus Christ for the inspiration and vision He has given me to press on.

# ABOUT THE AUTHOR

**B**RUCE LOEFFLER is president of the Enspiron Company. He holds a bachelor's degree in business and a master's degree in communications. He has taught service excellence at Texas Christian University, Fort Worth, and the University of Texas at Arlington, and business ethics at Dallas Baptist University.

Bruce began his career with Disneyland's "Kids of the Kingdom," a live performing group. He was then asked to move to Florida to perform and lead several other professional groups. At Disney World, he was given a unique opportunity to create a new position overseeing Showmanship Service for Epcot and the Magic Kingdom and also served as a supervisor in the Magic Kingdom.

His passion is to challenge, stretch, and motivate employees and leaders to excellence. Since leaving Disney World, he has helped improve service excellence in hospitals, Chrysler, Six Flags, CompUSA, supermarkets, department stores, airlines, banks, hotels, car dealerships, and other industries.

Bruce resides in Brentwood, Tennessee with his wife and two children. Information regarding speaking and training may be obtained at www.oneminuteservice.com, by emailing bruce@oneminuteservice.com, or by calling 877.407.7787.

# ATTITUDE *MAKES* THE

# DIFFERENCE

*Ability is what you are capable of doing.*
*Motivation determines what you do.*
*Attitude determines how well you do it.*

—LOU HOLTZ

WHAT IS IT THAT MAKES Disney World better than other theme parks? *Service.* And what makes Disney's service better than the service at just about every other park? *Attitude.* More than any other component, attitude is the key ingredient in the success of Walt Disney World cast members. It doesn't matter how smart, how talented, or even how attractive you are, without a good attitude you will *never* go very far at Disney World — or at any other company for that matter.

*Attitude is an outward expression of
internal feelings.*

The past twenty plus years have seen a general decline in the attitudes of employees. There is greater *disconnect* between employees and customers than ever before. Employees are often going through the motions and just "putting in their time." They don't seem to be genuinely interested in customers' needs. They give matter-of-fact or curt responses if they respond at all. One of the major concerns in business today is the lack of respect employees tend to show their customers and each other as well.

As mentioned in the *Introduction*, I had the incredible privilege of being a cast member at Disneyland and then at Walt Disney World before being asked to create a new position overseeing Showmanship Service for the Magic Kingdom and Epcot. My role was to develop the presentation skills of Disney cast members in the Attractions Division, attractions such as the Jungle Cruise, Space Mountain, and Spaceship Earth.

In the process, I discovered that some Disney cast members needed additional training, so I developed new programs to improve customer service, motivation, teamwork, communication, and leadership. As success of the training spread, so did word to other departments such as Merchandise, Foods, Tickets, Parking, and Guest Relations. Soon training was requested for these departments as well. It was the most challenging, yet the most rewarding job I've ever had.

I then spent over a year in the Casting Department. Casting selects new cast members for many of those same departments. During that year, I hired over 500 new cast members. The number one quality I always looked for was their *attitude and approach to work.* I continually looked for individuals who were positive, who liked people, who enjoyed helping others, and who worked at getting along with other people. Individuals with those qualities tended to be the most successful Disney World cast members.

The Dale Carnegie Foundation made an interesting discovery regarding how employees get ahead on the job: **15%** is due to their technical skills and knowledge, but **85%** is due to their attitude and people skills. It wasn't about *how do you get the job?* — you must have knowledge and skills to get the job. It was about *how do you get ahead?* You get ahead by your attitude, your people skills, and how well you get along with other people. Skills and knowledge can be learned, but *you* cannot change a person's personality or their attitude; he or she must change these on their own. ***Remember:*** If a person is negative or cynical by nature, there is a strong probability that he or she will always be negative and cynical unless they make a conscious decision to change. Attitude plays a critical role in how effective and successful a person will be on the job *and* throughout life.

A man had purchased an airline ticket. Weeks later he called the airline to reserve his seat. Unknown to him, the price had gone down by $250. But the man made a huge mistake: he was belligerent and rude to the ticket agent. Even though the man could have received the difference, the ticket agent chose not to tell him about it. When asked why she hadn't told him about the price change, the agent replied, "He was a jerk and didn't deserve it!" **Remember**: Your attitude also plays a major role in how others treat you in return.

*Attitude is the filter for everything you think, say, or do.*

Your attitude impacts every aspect of your job and your relationships with others. *You* choose the attitude you possess, whether it will be negative or positive. *You* display one or the other:

+ **A negative attitude:** using negative language; whining and complaining; criticizing customers or co-workers; taking your frustration out on others; feeling like a victim; and dwelling on problems rather than focusing on solutions

- **A positive attitude:** taking pride in your work; striving for excellence; giving your best; encouraging others; finding positive things to say about your work and others; and improving yourself, your co-workers, and the company you work for

If you were the owner of a company or the manager of a department, which type of employee would you most likely hire or promote? Which one would be most likely to succeed on the job? Which one would work best with others?

If I could challenge you to change one thing, without question that would be: *improve your attitude.* Your attitude impacts virtually everything you do. Having a positive attitude doesn't make you any better than another employee. It simply helps make you more effective and enables you to become more successful than other employees.

I'm sure you've heard the old saying, "You can take a horse to water, but you can't make him drink." I have an addendum to that saying: "You can take a horse to water and you can't make him drink, *but* you can put some salt in his oats." What happens when you put salt in his oats? It makes him thirsty. I'm not equating employees with horses, but it is our responsibility to give each of our co-workers the thirst, the desire, to do and to become their best. It all starts with attitude.

**A final thought.** After working with numerous organizations since leaving Walt Disney World, I am convinced that new employees, especially younger ones, need a mentor or an accountability partner to help them to become responsible, successful employees. Organizations that take the initiative to challenge, encourage, inspire, and help their employees improve tend to succeed. But those companies that leave their new employees to succeed or fail on their own are the companies that fail most often. At Disney, most cast members were initially partnered with a trainer or an individual whose job was to "show them the ropes" and help them succeed. That's another reason Disney World was so effective.

# A. ATTITUDE IS A CHOICE

*Attitude is what differentiates you*
*from your competition.*

You have a choice about how you interact with other people. A condescending attitude or negative words can be very offensive. Once said or done, they cannot be taken back. A bad or negative mood often controls how you behave. But your behavior can control your mood, so act the way you *would like to feel*. Put a smile on your face and focus on the positive aspects of your work!

1.   **Service is about retaining customers.** A successful business not only makes a profit, but it is also able to attract and retain customers. Customers are the lifeblood of every business and without them — especially repeat customers — a business cannot survive. Your level of service is often the factor that makes people return and tell their friends good things about your business. If you want to be successful, then you need to be effective at helping people. If you do not enjoy helping others, then the service industry might be the wrong profession for you.

2.   **You are responsible.** You alone are responsible for your attitude. You determine if your attitude is positive or negative and how you respond to others. No one can force you to be anything less than who you are *unless you allow them to*. Regardless of what others do or say, you have the power to *do the right thing*. Pleasing a customer who is determined to take their frustration and anger out on you can be extremely difficult — but each of us is responsible for creating a positive experience for every customer *no matter what*.

3. **Everything communicates.** One of the keys to Disney World's success is meticulous attention to detail. Just about everything imaginable is carefully planned, staged, and prepared for one thing: creating a positive guest experience. Disney strives to incorporate each of the human senses into the guest experience. The objective is to transport guests from the hustle and bustle of the outside world to a magical place where they can "get away," but it cannot be done without every cast member doing his or her part. Similarly, everything you do communicates to your customers as well: the appearance of the building, the trash in the parking lot and entrances, the background music, the attire of each employee, the cleanliness of the facility, the professionalism, how each customer perceives they are being treated, and the list goes on. Everything the customer sees, hears, tastes, smells, and experiences communicates. Take a good look at your facility. What does a customer see and sense? How well do employees present themselves? How effectively do *you* interact with customers? Ask yourself, "What does *my* attitude communicate to my customers?"

**4.** **Take personal pride in everything you do:**

+ **Take pride in your appearance.** Your appearance shows how much you care about yourself and your job. Is it professional or does it look sloppy?

+ **Take pride in your area.** Pick up trash, sweep, dust, and straighten your area. Make cleanliness, especially clean restrooms, a priority.

+ **Take pride in your work.** Your work is a reflection of you — the pride you have in yourself and the quality of your efforts.

+ **Take pride in your service.** How you serve others is also a reflection of you. Study ways to improve your people skills and learn how to best work with others effectively.

+ **Take pride in the paperwork you give to the public.** Never give a copy of a copy of a copy to a customer. Sloppy paperwork makes your company look second-class and cheap.

+ **Take pride in being excellent.** Challenge yourself to take on an attitude of excellence. Your boss and your customers expect it. The job you do is like signing a painting. It reflects on you and the pride you take in your work. For your own sake, give your best!

*We can alter our lives by altering our attitudes.*
—WILLIAM JAMES

5. **Feelings follow actions.** You can change how you feel by changing your behavior. Act the way you want to feel and you will begin to feel the way you are acting. Here's why it works. The mind is a neutral instrument. When you arrive at work in a bad mood, your mind senses your mood and promotes negative behavior. But when you *smile*, your mind senses that you want to change from a bad to a good mood and in a few hours you actually put yourself in a good mood. The key is to smile consistently for several hours, not just a few minutes. You can literally change how you feel by changing *what you think* and by changing *the expression on your face*! Try it — it works! **Remember**: It all starts with attitude and everything succeeds or fails from there.

6. **Create a positive experience.** See your business through your customers' eyes. Never deliberately give customers the runaround or inconvenience them. If you cannot find the answer, find someone who can, but never leave customers "hanging." Always put your customer's needs ahead of what you're doing. Remove any barriers that make it hard for the

customer to succeed. *Remember*: Especially in difficult economic times, customers have a choice. They don't *have to* do business with you; they can go somewhere else or go online. Think about this: if I buy a $500 suit at Macy's and return it, any clerk at the counter can cheerfully refund my money, but if I return an 89¢ candy bar to my local drug store, I must wait until a manager has time to come to the register and authorize the return. Which of these two companies trusts their employees and which company respects my time more?

Carl Sewell, owner of Sewell Village Lexus in Dallas, once commented: Over the course of a lifetime, a typical customer will spent $322,000 with us, so it doesn't make much sense to argue over a $50 part if we could lose $322,000 by offending them. Make doing business with you *easy*. What do customers want, need, and expect? What obstacles do your customers encounter that create a negative experience? How can obstacles be reduced or eliminated? *Remember*: Whatever you're not willing to do to satisfy customers, your competition probably is.

*Onstage is being excellent in everything
you do around the customer.*

11

7.    **Apply onstage and backstage.** Two of the most
      important concepts I learned at Disney World
      were *onstage* and *backstage*. They are great
      concepts you should consider incorporating
      into your organization as well. Simply put,
      anytime you are in an area where a customer
      can see or hear you, you are *onstage*. Anything
      that is visually intrusive, or an attitude that is
      less than positive or detracts from excellence,
      should *not* be in an onstage area. When you
      are onstage, you are expected to be at your
      best, to be knowledgeable about your products
      and services, and to keep your area looking
      great. *Onstage* is about excellence in everything
      you do around the customer. *Backstage* is where
      you can let your guard down *a bit*. Backstage
      is any area away from the customer. Places
      such as a back room, a storage area, delivery
      areas, and break rooms are usually out of the
      view of customers. For instance, the entrance
      of your business would be an onstage area.
      So taking a smoking break in front of your
      building would look unprofessional and is
      *not acceptable*. **Remember**: The entrance to
      your building is where customers often form
      their first impression of your business.

8.    **The #1 negative attitude in service today
      is apathy.** According to the survey in the

*Introduction*, 68% of people stop doing business with a company because they believe the company or the employees just don't care! Apathy — an *I don't care, it's not my job*, or *that's not my problem* attitude — kills business and destroys trust. Apathy is a self-centered attitude that says *I couldn't care less about you, your needs, or your feelings. I'm only concerned with myself*, and customers hate it! Apathetic employees simply go through the motions of doing their jobs, but with no feeling, energy, or purpose. On the surface, apathy might seem somewhat harmless, but in reality apathetic employees are detrimental to the success of a company! Apathy has some close "cousins" that are just as destructive: *indifference, complacency, ambivalence,* and *ignoring* others. We display these attitudes, often without knowing it, to our customers, co-workers, and even our families. Sometimes it's difficult to smile, be friendly, and have a pleasant personality the entire day, but you still have to. If you desire to succeed and be the kind of person others want to do business with, avoid apathy at all cost.

*Never tell people your problems.*
*90% of them don't care and the other*
*10% are actually glad you have them!*

9. **Kill the blame and excuses.** Most customers aren't interested in hearing about your problems and frustrations — they want results. Customers don't care that you're short-staffed, that Mary is sick or Jim is late, or that you didn't get a lunch break when you were supposed to. When you blame others or make excuses, you are ultimately refusing to take responsibility for the success of your department. To your customer, there are no excuses! One of the most destructive things in any business is an individual who is cynical and critical of everything and everyone. People who are critical, cynical, and sarcastic undermine morale. A cynical attitude pulls you and your co-workers down and creates a very negative impression of you and your company. Dave Ramsey, a financial guru on radio and television, offers some practical advice for running a successful business: "Stop the gossip and rumors!" Gossip and rumors negatively impact people and destroy respect, the team, support, cooperation, self-esteem, and effectiveness. My advice: stay away from individuals who are negative, cynical, and destructive. The bottom

line is: if you are unhappy in your job, either change your attitude or find something else you like to do! You're not a rock; you're not a tree. You can change, but all change *must begin with you*.

10.  **Avoid these attitudes:**

- **Never criticize the three C's:** c̲ustomers, c̲ompetition, or c̲o-workers. Negative comments often return and *will be* used against you one day.

- **Never "brush off" a customer.** Don't use short, curt responses or approaches. Doing so implies that you aren't really interested in them.

- **Never argue or yell at a customer.** You cannot win by insulting or fighting with a customer. Politely excuse yourself and ask a manager to take over.

- **Never curse or swear around a customer.** Cursing and swearing are offensive! They degrade the customer's image of you and your company.

- **Never be sarcastic, condescending, or callous with a customer.** Nothing they have done warrants your cynicism, arrogance, or sarcasm.

- **Never chew gum around a customer.** Chewing gum looks *tacky*. Use a breath mint so customers can't see you chewing on anything.

- **Don't pass the buck.** Customers get frustrated when they get the runaround and no one will help them solve their problem.

## B. KEEP IT POSITIVE

*There is little difference in people,*
*but that little difference makes a big difference.*
*The little difference is attitude ...*
*the big difference is whether it is positive or*
*negative.*

—W. CLEMENT STONE

Negativity just comes naturally to many people. From experience I've found that it's five times easier to be negative than to be positive. The individuals who seem to succeed in life are almost always positive people. Somehow they can turn negative situations into positive ones. Be the one who sees a difficult customer as an opportunity to improve your own skills to turn the customer's situation around.

11. **Focus on the positive aspects of your job.** Be a person who builds up people. Anyone can be

negative and anyone can tear down other people, but the way you see people determines how you treat them. I once worked for a company that used seasonal employees during the summer months. I was surprised that some employees and supervisors called seasonal employees some of the worst names you can imagine behind their backs. Equally disappointing was the way in which those same employees and supervisors treated those seasonal employees. Be the person who builds people up, not one who tears them down.

12. **Realize that you are 100% responsible for your success.** Your problem isn't your boss, it isn't your co-workers, it isn't even your customers — it's *you!* You can't blame the government, the economy, gas prices, your job, your boss, or even your customers for your lack of success. Life is about choices. You ultimately determine where you go and what you do. Bad things happen to everyone. It's really not so much about what happens to you — it's about what *you do about* what happens to you that counts. People who fail tend to see problems as brick walls, while successful people see them as speed bumps that are only a minor distraction in their day. You are 100% responsible for your

success or failure. It does not help to blame others or to feel as though you are a victim. Instead, take your future "by the horns" and do something positive with it.

13. **Negativity is contagious.** Negativity kills cooperation, respect, pride, and the desire others may have to work with you. Have you ever met someone who is negative about everything? Doesn't it seem as though a huge black cloud follows them everywhere they go and then zaps them? If you ever have the opportunity to work next to a negative person, don't just walk away — *RUN!* It's true. You do become what you associate with. If you want to change how you think and improve your work habits, start associating with people who have a positive attitude and great work ethics and stop hanging around with people who pull you down and bring out the worst in you. You might have to fight to stay positive, but it is well worth the effort.

## C. BE YOUR BEST

*Average never inspired anyone!*

No one can be average *and* excellent. As long as you are willing to settle for average, you will never achieve excellence. Average has never inspired you or anyone else to greatness, but excellence has and does.

14. **Be professional.** *Look the part.* A major part of your job is to always look professional. Before you go to work, make certain your clothes are clean and ironed, your shoes are polished, and you have washed and combed your hair. Wear a smile. If you have a name tag, wear it. When I worked at Disney World, if you did not have a name tag, you could not start work until you had one. In business today, your ID offers security for the customer as well as a way for them to connect with you instantly. *Act the part.* A professional does not dwell on petty things. They don't make time for it. Professionals present an image of confidence and self-control. They believe in themselves and see customers and co-workers as part of their team and do whatever it takes to support and help their team win.

15. **Cleanliness is essential.** Have you ever wondered how Walt Disney World can keep 28,000 acres so clean, yet your local convenience store can't keep clutter off their tiny parking lot? Here's how Disney does it: every cast member at Disney World is expected to pick up trash whenever they see it. That's the only way Disney can keep the property so clean

— everyone pitches in and does their part. I remember walking down Main Street in the Magic Kingdom. A discarded drink cup was on the sidewalk about 20 feet to my right. After I passed it, a manager stopped me and said, "You passed right by that cup. Why didn't you pick it up?" I said, "I'm sorry, but I didn't see it." He then responded, "It's your job to always look for trash and pick it up." I can tell you that from then on, I looked for paper and cups and anything else that looked like trash! It works the same way at your company as well. Your business will never achieve an image of excellence unless every employee takes the ownership to pick up trash when he or she sees it; to clean off counters in the restrooms; and to take care of anything else that detracts from the appearance of your facility.

*Tomorrow is an outgrowth and
a byproduct of today.*

16. **Never settle for mediocrity**. Understand that each day you lay the foundation for your future. Today is the foundation of tomorrow. If you plan to be excellent tomorrow, then you had better be excellent today. Good gets you by in most companies, but as long as you are willing

to settle for *good*, you will never reach *excellence*. Just because others around you settle for second best, why would you? Excellence must begin with you. Excellence is about being your best, no matter what you do and no matter where you are. Make the choice to be excellent. Never settle for mediocrity!

17. **Be 1% better today than you were yesterday.** Everyday, make it your goal to be 1% better at who you are and what you do. Most of us do not grow in quantum leaps. We tend to grow in incremental steps. Baby steps help us grow a little today and a little more tomorrow as we continually lay new foundations on those baby steps. Just imagine what would happen if you applied just this one principle. Think about the tremendous personal growth you would achieve *in just one year*.

## Essential Ideas from the Attitude Key

If you can improve only one thing, by all means *change your attitude*. Most bosses will not tell you that it was your attitude that kept you from getting the promotion, the pay raise, or the job in the first place, but it often is. There are excellent books, CDs, and DVDs by experts who can help you improve your attitude and improve your life. Get them, study them, and use them. Apply the tools that will propel you to being exceptional. *Remember*: Attitude is the *foundation* of everything you think, say, and do.

## Attitude is a choice.

+ Take pride in everything you do. Give your best.
+ The #1 attitude that destroys service is apathy.
+ Apply onstage and backstage to your service.

## Keep it positive.

+ It is five times easier to be negative than positive.
+ Realize that you are 100% responsible for your success.
+ Never criticize customers, competition, or co-workers.

## Be your best.

+ You cannot be average and also be excellent.
+ Keep your area looking clean. Pick up trash.
+ Be 1% better today than you were yesterday.

# 2

## G — THE GREET KEY

*People tend to form an opinion of you
within the first seven seconds.*

G — THE FIRST KEY OF GREAT Service, is to **Greet** every customer who enters your business or area when you first see them. How you greet customers the first time often determines their perception of you and your company — either positive or negative. The goal of the **Greet** key is to establish a positive first impression with every customer you come in contact with. At Disney, I used the term *guest perception* in order to help cast members understand service from the guest's perspective. For a guest, the effectiveness of a Disney cast member was determined by the guest's perception of them: their attitude, their level of pride and professionalism, how knowledgeable they were, and how much they genuinely cared. All of these were part of *guest perception*. Your customers focus on many of the same areas in your business as well.

In his book *You Are the Message*, Roger Ailes states that people formulate first impressions in the first seven seconds. He simply reinforces what many others have discovered: it only takes a few seconds to leave a lasting impression. Those first few seconds have the power to set a positive or negative image of your company; and much of it depends on you and how well you greet your customers.

I continue to be surprised at the lack of interest some employees express in helping customers. Having a *this is just a job* mentality doesn't cut it! Those employees must not realize that most customers can easily tell when they're bored or don't care and are there just for a paycheck. The boss might sign your paycheck, but he or she doesn't pay your salary. The customer does and he or she can fire you anytime they please. Customers fire you by choosing not to return to your business and they tell their friends and family to shop elsewhere as well.

*Great service isn't rocket science.*
*It's the science of how we treat people.*

GREAT Service is more than simply doing an excellent job at the basics. Woody Allen once said, "80% of success is just showing up." Success takes a little more than just showing up, but Mr. Allen has a point. A couple of years ago, I was training some employees and I asked the group, "What specific things do you do to provide exceptional service to your customers?" One young man spoke up: "I come to work everyday!" Many employees are present *physically*, they show up, but they are somewhere else *mentally*. Their focus is not on their jobs and it's a long way from the needs of the customer.

In Chapter 1, we discussed the importance of attitude and striving for excellence in whatever you do. In order to be excellent, you must continue to improve yourself and develop your skills. When you're at work, give your 100%! Put your best into everything you do. Your focus should not be on your co-workers, but on yourself and the level of excellence you provide. If you consistently strive to be excellent at the basics, develop a positive attitude, and improve your performance, you will do a great job and excel in whatever you do.

Ann went to an upscale store to purchase a sweater. The clerk behind the counter was busy working on her computer, so Ann asked where the sweaters were. Without looking up, the clerk motioned to her right and said, "In the tops section." Ann found the sweater she wanted, but couldn't find a fitting room, so she returned to the clerk and asked where the fitting rooms were. The clerk motioned to her left. Ann then found the doors in the fitting rooms were locked. Again she returned to the clerk to inquire about unlocking the doors. The clerk tossed a key at her from behind the counter and continued working on her computer. Ann tried on the sweater and returned to the clerk. This time she was quite agitated and said, "Ma'am, would you please look at me! Who is your store manager?" The surprised clerk looked up and said, "I am. Is there a problem?" Ann said, "You have been the rudest, most disinterested person I have ever encountered and I will never be back!" Less than a year later that store went out of business. I wonder why.

There is no magic formula for providing GREAT Service, but *yagottawanna*! No one can be forced to provide great service or to have an excellent attitude. You have to want to do it. At Disney World, one of my goals was to help each cast member find the *want to* for themselves: to challenge them to fine-tune their talents and abilities in order to create a positive and enjoyable experience for every Disney guest.

## *YOU are the company.*

For customers, their first impression is instrumental in forming their overall perception of you and their overall impression of your company. I'm sure you've heard the expression, "You never get a second chance to make a first impression." It's true. About

G — THE GREET KEY

80% of the perception customers form of a company is based on their initial impression of the employees they encounter.

At Disney World, a guest encounters about 70 cast members in a typical day. Those encounters provide 70 opportunities to create a positive or negative impression. Each cast member needs to understand an important principle: to that guest, YOU are Disney World! The same is true of your company as well. It doesn't matter if you work for McDonalds, Sears, a bank, a restaurant, or a car dealership — to the customer, YOU are the company. How you greet customers "sets the tone." That's why first impressions, especially from those who answer the telephone, are so important. If you do a poor job greeting customers or sound cold and apathetic on the telephone, the direct message you send to the caller is: "We really don't care." Ask yourself: would I trust a business that sounds disinterested over the telephone?

Common courtesies and respect seem to be rapidly disappearing from service today. Too many employees seem as though they really don't care. They don't appear to take pride in their work. Perhaps poor service is just a reflection of what we see around us everyday. It's offensive when employees ignore customers, go through the motions, or are rude and discourteous. The solution: it takes only about five seconds to apply the **Greet** key and set a positive tone for your customers!

## A. WELCOME THEM

One of the many things Disney World does effectively is greeting guests. At many attractions and restaurants, Disney utilizes a greeter. The primary job of a greeter is to welcome each guest and to direct them where they should go next. Greeters also provide information, such as how long the wait time will be or what the attraction is about. Take a look at your company. How can you incorporate a greeter in your business to assist customers and create a positive first impression of your company?

*Make every customer feel as welcome*
*as you would a guest in your home.*

18. **Treat customers as guests.** One of the best ideas I learned from Disney was to treat every customer as though they were a guest in my home. That's why Disney never uses the term *customer*. At Disney, customers are called *guests* because a guest tends to be viewed in a little different light than a customer. Here is the logic behind the terminology. If you invite valued friends for dinner or to visit your home, what

would you do in preparation for their visit? You would probably clean your home and maybe bake some cookies and put on a pot of coffee. When they come to the door, you would greet them and make them feel welcome. You would do everything you could to make their visit pleasant and enjoyable. It's the same in your business as well. Treating customers as guests is an excellent philosophy. If every employee in your company would view customers as special guests, in the same way they would guests in their home, customers would leave with an excellent impression of you and your company.

19. **Smile! It's a nice reflection on you.** Smiling is one of the best ways to create a positive impression. What other body language tells people about the kind of mood you are in, if you are having a good day, or if you like being around people *any better* than your smile? When you smile and when it's genuine, you tell people that you are friendly and positive and that you are glad to see them. A smile also conveys that you enjoy what you do. A sincere smile is one of the most effective ways to present a positive image of yourself to customers and to your co-workers. *Remember:* When you smile and do it consistently, it will change your mood

and improve your day, plus you'll be much more enjoyable to be around.

20. **Make good eye contact.** Although a smile is essential to show friendliness and warmth, your eyes reveal sincerity and help you to connect with others. In our culture, the foundation of trust begins with good eye contact. If someone will not look you in the eye, are you likely to trust them? *Probably not.* Good eye contact expresses your feelings about others and helps build trust between you and the other person. It also shows the level of confidence that you have in yourself. The lack of direct eye contact makes customers feel uncomfortable and doubt your sincerity.

# B. INITIATE THE INTERACTION

*It is your job to make every customer feel welcome and important.*

Customers can usually sense if you're interested in helping them. Initiate the interaction and do whatever you can to make every customer feel welcome as soon as possible.

21. **Apply the ten-foot rule.** When you come within ten feet of customers, be the first to

initiate the interaction. When you first meet a customer, greet him or her with eye contact and a smile. Whenever possible, greet customers with a handshake, pay a compliment, include the family, and use small talk. Never avert your eyes by looking at the ceiling or floor when you pass by a customer. The ten-foot rule also applies to your co-workers as well. When you see a co-worker, acknowledge him, give him eye contact, and always show interest in him. The ten-foot rule is an excellent guide to help each employee create a positive first impression of themselves and your company.

22. **Welcome them.** Your job is to create an inviting, welcoming place where customers want to do business. Make customers glad they chose to do business with your company. Welcome them with a cheerful *good morning, thank you for coming in,* or *may I help you?* If a customer looks lost or asks about something, offer to help or say, *I'll be glad to take you there* and take them to their destination. Yes, it takes two or three minutes of your time, but it's a great way to show that you genuinely care about them. *Remember:* The greeting you give a customer forms their initial impression of you and your company that day, so make it a positive one.

*Nothing great was ever accomplished*
*without enthusiasm.*

—RALPH WALDO EMERSON

23. **Use energy and enthusiasm.** If it wouldn't bore
you, I would discuss the importance of energy
and enthusiasm in every chapter of this book!
Using energy and enthusiasm in your voice is
*that* important! I believe it! Can you imagine
Thomas Edison, Henry Ford, Martin Luther
King, or Thomas Jefferson without passion?
Enthusiasm differentiates you from others.
At Disney World, one of my responsibilities
was to work with the cast members who made
live presentations to guests. One of the things
I worked on was getting cast members to
use their voices to convey interest in their
message. I was surprised by just how many
cast members did not have a clue about how
their voices impacted their presentations. The
consistent phrase I used was, "You need to put
some energy and enthusiasm in your voice."
Using energy and enthusiasm in your voice
communicates confidence and confidence
translates into trust.

24. **Don't be plastic.** Customers can usually tell
when you are being plastic or faking it. When

you go through the motions, you come across as insincere. Here's an example. What is your typical response when someone asks, *How are you doing?* The majority of us say *fine* and most of the time it's a plastic response. The word *fine* is often a brush-off phrase. When people ask me, *How are you doing?* I never say fine. I say *terrific, super, excellent, awful,* or *great.* I try to stay away from fine because I think it's plastic. Rather than being plastic, why not be sincere and genuine? About this time you're thinking, "But when the other person says, 'How are you doing?' they don't care either, so why should I?" It's not about *other people* — it's about *you,* your attitude and your level of excellence! You are accountable for what you say and how you say it. If you want to break out of the rut of being plastic, begin by being genuine in your responses and your approach to others. Zig Ziglar is a motivational speaker who often uses the word "terrific" when asked how he is doing. Someone once asked Zig if he always feels terrific. Zig replied, "No, I'm just forecasting how I intend to feel." What a great outlook on life! Use responses that reflect how you feel or at least how you *intend* to feel.

## C. PHONE SETS THE TONE

*How you answer the telephone is critical to how others see you and your company.*

At Disney World, I also worked with hundreds of cast members on the importance of adding inflection and personality to their voices. People who speak in a monotone voice, without inflection, come across to the listener as being either apathetic or bored. Inflection is the upward and downward motion that gives your voice warmth and personality. It's what makes you sound interesting and engaged rather than dull and boring.

Avoid using automated answering systems whenever possible. Automated systems sound robotic and can make your company seem impersonal and out of touch with the customer. People hate talking to an unresponsive machine. Always opt for a live, friendly person to answer the telephone over an automated system. Also make sure you return calls. Recently I heard a startling statistic: 72% of leaders do not return their telephone calls or emails in a timely manner, if at all!

25. **Inflection gives your voice personality.** How you use your voice is very important. According to Dr. Albert Mehrabian, a communications

expert from UCLA, communication typically consists of three parts:

+ 7% are the words we use.

+ 38% is vocal: tone of voice, inflection, style, volume, and personality.

+ 55% is body language: eyes, mouth, head, hands, body, and posture.

Over the telephone, there is no body language, so the percentages increase:

+ 14% are the words we say.

+ 86% is the tone of voice we use.

When you speak, use warmth and enthusiasm in your voice so you sound interesting rather than mundane and bored.

26. **Answer by the third ring.** Make every attempt to answer all telephone calls by the third ring, if not sooner. Respect the caller's time when they call you. I once called a company and it took exactly four and a half minutes before anyone answered! When I finally spoke to the operator, I asked why it had taken so long. She sarcastically snapped, "We're busy!" After the call and the operator's response, I started thinking about the perceptions other callers might have of this company:

- They're really swamped. They're too busy to help me.

- They're understaffed. Employees must be stressed out.

- Management doesn't care and neither do employees.

- Employees don't receive the training or support they need.

- Employees must feel disrespected and under-appreciated.

The accuracy of these perceptions isn't the issue. It's the perceptions themselves that are important. Make it a priority to always answer your telephone by the third ring to demonstrate the value you place on callers.

27. **Put a smile in your voice.** How you answer the telephone makes an important impression on a caller. Be professional and courteous and set a *positive tone* on the telephone. A physical smile translates into an emotional smile over the telephone. When you smile when answering the telephone, you will sound more friendly, caring, and professional. The caller can hear emotion over a telephone. They can hear happy, sad, positive, helpful, frustrated, angry, and a myriad of other emotions, whether you intend

to convey them or not. It's also important to put a smile in your voice. A smile on your face results in a positive reflection of you.

28. **Four steps to answering the telephone.** How you answer the telephone says a lot about you and your company. Make every effort to use a well-trained, friendly person to answer the telephone in order to give your company a positive "personality." One time I called a company and the person answered the telephone with a nasty, "Yeah, wha da ya want!" Either he had caller ID and was already mad at me or he was having a really bad day. His response set a bad tone for the rest of our conversation and created a poor image of his company. Your greeting should reflect your personality and professionalism. Greetings should last between three and five seconds, period. Much longer and callers can become impatient, but any shorter than three seconds doesn't give callers enough information. But don't rush or speed through the greeting. The information is for a caller's benefit, so say it clearly, distinctly, and add warmth and personality to your voice. The following four steps are an excellent model for answering the telephone:

1. **Give a positive greeting.** Say *good morning, afternoon, evening* or *thank you for calling.*

2. **Identify the company or your department.** Let them know which company or department they have reached.

3. **Introduce yourself.** Use your first name. It is more personable and helps you to connect with a caller more quickly.

4. **Offer assistance.** Say, *How may I assist you?* Then direct them to the right person.

These four steps take less than four seconds, yet they help create a positive image of your company and help employees be more personable, consistent, and professional.

## Essential Ideas from the Greet Key

It is essential to create a positive impression immediately. The first key of GREAT Service is to **Greet** every customer when you first meet them. You should initiate the interaction and make customers feel welcome. A genuine smile and good eye contact are an excellent start. Also, how you answer the telephone tells the caller volumes about you and your company. *Remember:* to the customer, YOU are the company.

## Welcome them.

+ Treat customers as guests visiting your home.

+ Apply the ten-foot rule. Greet customers within ten feet.

+ Smile, give good eye contact, and be friendly and personable.

## Initiate the interaction.

+ Say *good morning, good afternoon,* or *good evening.*

+ Say *thank you for coming in* or *may I help you?*

+ Always use energy and enthusiasm in what you say.

## Phone sets the tone.

+ Inflection gives your voice more personality.

+ A smile in your voice makes you sound friendly.

+ Apply the four steps each time you answer the telephone.

# 3

# R — THE RELATE KEY

*Given the choice, people will always do business
with people they can connect with.*

R — THE SECOND KEY OF GREAT Service,
is to **Relate**. The **Relate** key helps you
connect with every customer in order to
build rapport with them. Service is really about relationships. Connecting is important because it takes
an *impersonal* relationship to a more *personal* level.
The time and effort you spend relating to customers
builds a foundation for the trust and confidence that
they have in you and your company. That confidence
translates into repeat and even lifelong customers.
Your goal should be to have a positive experience
with *every* customer by connecting and building rapport with them, even if the service interaction lasts
only a few seconds.

I've been told that about 70% of Disney guests
are repeat customers. How well you relate to your

customers determines their perception of you, your company, and your products or service. Seek to build a foundation for a long-term relationship with each customer. In other words, treat *each* customer as though you expect them to be a *customer for life*.

One of my pet peeves is *disconnected* employees! When I go to a supermarket or a department store, I'm often surprised at how out of touch some employees seem to be with their customers. At the local supermarket checkout counter, frequently there is no greeting, little eye contact, and almost no interaction from the cashier other than to tell me how much I owe. After receiving my change, rarely is there an appreciative *thank you* or *come again* — just a mundane *Have a nice day — next!* The cashier moves on to the next customer and repeats the process. I'm certain most customers get tired of the plastic service they receive in businesses today.

I recently heard a story about Jay Leno, former host of *The Tonight Show*. When Jay went through a supermarket check-out line, the cashier was not very friendly and she didn't say *thank you* when she finished his transaction. As he left, Jay commented about her not having the courtesy to thank him for his business. She sarcastically responded, "It's printed on your receipt!" Unless *you* make an effort, the service you give customers will be boring and impersonal.

Another pet peeve is receiving a robotic response when an employee answers the telephone with, "What is your account number?" When will companies wake up and realize how impersonal words like these are and that they cause customers to feel like they're insignificant — and that their customers hate it? Why not simply answer the telephone pleasantly with one of the following:

+ "Hello, my name is Jim with ABC Company. With whom do I have the pleasure of speaking?"

+ "Thank you for calling, Mary, my name is Jim. In order to be of better assistance, may I have your account number?"

+ "Thank you for calling. This is Jim, how may I help you today?"

Expressing genuine interest in a customer, even if only for a few seconds on the telephone, helps you relate to them as a person rather than as an adversary. When each employee takes a genuine interest in customers and makes an effort to connect with them, customers will be far more receptive and cooperative.

Although getting to know your customer is important, there is no "one size fits all" formula. Customers come in all shapes, sizes, personalities, and temperaments, so it's necessary to hone your observational skills to determine their moods. But before analyzing a customer, take a moment to put yourself in their shoes. Think carefully about how you would want to be treated.

The **Relate** key is about connecting with customers by building rapport with them and creating relationships that turn them into life-time customers. When you work with customers, you must be at your best. Put your personal issues on the back burner for the time being. Although it is difficult to be a professional when you have personal concerns, you still need to maintain your focus, have a pleasant personality, and take care of your customers' needs. Use the **Relate** key to get to know your customers, their likes, their dislikes, and what they want. In many cases, you only have a few seconds to connect with them. Even when you're busy, the **Relate** key can be executed in as few as ten seconds.

## A. CONNECT WITH THEM

*The biggest insult you can give another person*
*is to ignore them.*

If I call you a name or insult your intelligence, I am still treating you as a person, but if I ignore you, I am treating you as a non-person or an object. Here's an interesting question: what is the opposite of love? If you answered *hate*, then you would agree with the majority of other people. Love and hate are not opposite, but somewhat parallel feelings. The opposite of love is not hate, but *indifference*. How many times have you ignored someone, acted indifferently, or been apathetic, complacent, or callous toward another person and thought nothing of it? It probably happens more often than you think.

Connecting with customers helps you to *read* them. Everything you do or say, and even what you don't, communicates to customers. When you are reading customers, look for various clues. Do they seem relaxed or tense? Are they "just looking" or do they need help? Good conversation skills begin with your ability to relate to the customer on his or her level. Listen not only to what a customer says, but also to his or her tone of voice. Does he sound friendly? Does she sound agitated or simply in a hurry? Connecting helps you relate to customers on *their* level.

29. **Focus on building rapport and establishing relationships.** Make an effort to learn something about a customer so that you can connect with them. Your responsibility is to create an atmosphere that helps customers feel at home. Rapport with customers is best established by using small talk. Small talk is simply "breaking the ice" in order to get to know your customers better. It helps them feel at ease. Getting to know your customers helps establish long-term relationships and long-term relationships encourage customers to become repeat customers. Successful businesses depend on repeat customers.

30. **Make satisfying customers your first priority.** Create a strong bond with customers so they have little desire to go anywhere else. Always have their best interests in mind. Jim stayed at a hotel and ate dinner at the hotel's restaurant. He asked for two refills of his Coke, assuming that refills were free. When his bill came, he had been charged an additional 50¢ for each of the refills. Jim asked the restaurant manager to remove the additional charges because he hadn't been informed about them, but the

restaurant manager refused. Jim then asked for the hotel manager, who refused as well. Out of frustration, Jim contacted the corporate office of the hotel when he returned home. The corporate office not only refunded the additional $1 refill charge, but they also refunded the $150 cost of his room and charged it back to the hotel! Had the restaurant manager simply refunded the $1 refill charge, the hotel would have saved $150 and not lost a future guest and everyone else who heard Jim's story. Your question should always be: what's best for the customer? Then do it. *Remember:* The primary goal is not to make a profit, but to satisfy customers so they return and tell their friends about your business.

31. **Co-workers are customers too.** Use the same level of respect and appreciation with your co-workers as you use with your customers. Some employees never receive thanks from anyone. They rarely feel appreciated for the work they do. Your co-workers deserve to be treated with respect and appreciation. Serving customers and taking care of problems is tough enough, but without the support of your co-workers, problem situations will be even more difficult. I recently learned about Quality Living (QLI), an excellent company in Omaha,

Nebraska. QLI specializes in caring for patients with head injuries who come from all across the United States. In addition to providing superb medical care, QLI uses an unusual approach with their staff. Employees are treated as extended family. The QLI commitment doesn't end when employees clock out. QLI offers employee support for personal finance issues, counseling, drug and alcohol rehab, and a variety of other non-work-related concerns. QLI believes that by investing in each employee and making him or her as successful in their personal lives as they are at work, employees can be even more effective at work. Employees often say they feel "treated as gold" and never want to leave! It should come as no surprise that there is a long waiting list to get a job at QLI — and many are sharp people from non-medical fields.

# B. BUILD A RELATIONSHIP

*You determine how others perceive you and how you see them.*

Strive to build a positive relationship with customers. The key is to be friendly. Consider their needs before your own and you will change how they respond to you.

32. **Create a positive atmosphere.** GREAT Service is about creating a positive customer experience, regardless of the customer's attitude or mood. You are not responsible for their attitude, but you are responsible for the atmosphere you create in your department. Create one that is positive and friendly. Jean was shopping at a well-known department store. She was greeted by a very friendly, helpful employee who offered assistance. The employee helped Jean find the two items she had asked about. Jean was so pleased by the excellent service she had received that she went to the store manager's office to tell him about it. In the manager's office Jean met a secretary who asked what she needed. Jean asked, "May I please speak with the store manager?" The secretary snapped, "You have to fill out this complaint form first!" Jean politely responded, "But it's not about a complaint. I just wanted to compliment one of your employees for the excellent job she did." The secretary paused and said, "Well, we don't have a form for that." Isn't it strange how often we expect the worst, but rarely anticipate the best? Create a positive atmosphere by being friendly, helpful, positive, and cooperative.

33. **Look for something positive to think and say.** Never criticize other people. In the movie "Bambi," Thumper said something that has always stuck with me: *If you can't say somethin' nice, don't say nothin' at all.* Life at work and away from work will always go much smoother if you become a person who always has something positive to say. If you want to improve relationships, change what you say to the people you encounter. Every person has positive attributes — some you just have to look a little harder to find! If you can't find something positive to say, keep your comments to yourself. *Remember:* Better to be thought a fool than to open your mouth and remove all doubt.

34. **Add SPICE©: Five tips for relating to people.** In my training courses, I suggest some guidelines for effective service. One of my rules is: "You don't have the right to be negative or critical of another person the first time you meet them that day." Creating positive relationships with your customers and especially your co-workers is vitally important. I've developed the acronym SPICE to remind you of five things that will help build relationships. If you consistently apply SPICE to your customers and other

relationships, you will change how you see others and how they see you:

+ **S — Smile.** Ever heard the expression, *fake it 'til you make it?* Even if you don't feel like smiling, do it anyway.

+ **P — be Positive.** Anyone can be negative and critical. Look for positive things to say about everyone you meet, especially your co-workers.

+ **I — be Interested.** Take a genuine interest in everyone. Treat each person as if he or she were important. Learn about their wants and needs.

+ **C — Communicate.** Let customers know that you value them. Let what you say and do show that you genuinely care about them.

+ **E — be Encouraging.** Look for ways to inspire and build up others. Do whatever you can to create a positive experience for customers.

# C. PERSONALIZE YOUR SERVICE

*Take a personal interest in every person you meet.*

Have you ever had an injury, a serious illness, or had someone close to you die? What did you typically hear when someone expressed concern or sympathy? Was it, "If you need anything, just let me know?" How many times did you call them? The words *just let me know what I can do* sound helpful, but here's the problem: the person who is suffering is the one who must initiate the request for help, not the person who offered the assistance. Wouldn't it have been far more beneficial to say: "I'm bringing your supper tonight. What would you prefer, chicken or steak?" *Just let me know what I can do* are simply words. Telling a person what you will do and giving them simple options are action words. Which approach is more compassionate? When personalizing your service, *you* should initiate the action that does something to benefit the other person.

35. **Take a personal interest in other people.** There's an expression that goes, "People don't care how much you know until they know how much you care." It's true. Look for ways to demonstrate that you are genuinely concerned about other people. Do everything you can to

R — THE RELATE KEY

demonstrate interest in customers and what they need. One of the best ways to do this is to focus on them and offer to help with their selection. Follow up to ensure they are satisfied. On the way to work, Barb stopped at the drive-through of a local coffee shop for a cup of hot coffee. As she drove away she sipped the coffee and found that it was cold. When she arrived at work, she had to reheat it in the office microwave. The next time she went to the drive-through, she mentioned that her last cup of coffee had been cold and to please be sure this one was hot. The attendant apologized profusely. She also said, "This cup is on the house and here's a coupon for your next one." Barb said, "I didn't ask for anything. I just wanted a freshly poured cup of coffee. She seemed genuinely interested in me and made me feel that she really cared."

36. **The most important sound to anyone is hearing their name.** People who have the gift of remembering names have a distinct advantage over people who can only ask, "How ya doin'?" Make a special effort to learn and use customers' names. It helps you connect with them more quickly. Here is a good rule of thumb: always use Mr. or Mrs. and their last name unless you have permission to use another name. When I

was at a restaurant recently, a waitress referred to me as *sugar, honey,* and *sweetie* — all in the same sentence. Unless a customer has indicated that you may do so, don't use pet names like *honey* and *sweetie.* Some people like it and some don't. Don't automatically assume they do. Also, saying *hey you* is impersonal. If you don't know their name, use *sir* or *ma'am* to get their attention.

37. **Use your first name.** One of the most important principles I learned at Disney was that *everyone is important.* Many people like to use titles with their names, but titles before or after a name tend to create invisible barriers between you and your customers. To bridge the gap, Disney applied a simple solution: no matter who you are, always use your first name. Using first names does not detract from your professionalism, but it is especially effective when introducing yourself or relating to a customer. Using your first name actually helps you connect with customers more quickly and eliminates barriers.

38. **Listening connects you to other people.** Everyone has a need to be understood and to feel important. Several years ago I heard a comment on the radio that I thought was odd. The host said, "The greatest way to

demonstrate you love someone is to sincerely, genuinely listen to them." I thought, "that's baloney." Yet, as I thought about his comment, I realized that he was right. Listening is one of the best ways to show that you really care about a person. When you genuinely listen, you devote 100% of your attention to the other person. It tells them they're important. In a recent election, a friend of mine met both candidates within a short time period. He said, "The first candidate shook my hand, but seemed to be looking past me. He never made direct eye contact. I felt like he was searching the crowd for someone more important. The second candidate shook my hand and gave me his undivided attention for nearly 30 seconds. One made me feel insignificant and the other made me feel important." When you listen, give a person your full attention. Let them know that nothing or no one else is more important than they are *at that moment*. Here are some ideas to improve your listening skills:

+ **Give your undivided attention.** Make direct eye contact. Stop what you are doing and concentrate on the person and what they are saying.

+ **Ask questions that are related to the subject.** Some call this "active listening," which means to summarize and repeat information. Asking questions ensures that you are listening, understanding, and are on the "same page."

+ **Don't interrupt.** Interrupting can cause the speaker to feel that you think your idea is more important than his or that you aren't really interested.

+ **Complete the interaction and have an action plan.** Say *thank you* and make a comment that lets her know what you're going to do with the information.

## Essential Ideas from the Relate Key

The second key of GREAT Service enables you to **Relate** to the customer. Get to know your customers, their likes, their dislikes, and their wants. Relating enables you to connect with the customer and build a rapport. Few businesses can survive with one-time customers; they rely on repeat business. Your goal is to build a relationship and treat every customer as if they were a customer for life.

## Connect with them.

+ Use small talk to build a rapport with each customer.

+ Put customers first. Make their satisfaction your priority.

+ Give your co-workers the same respect you give customers.

## Build a relationship.

+ To change how customers see you, apply SPICE:

    + **Smile** whether you feel like it or not.

    + Be **Positive**. Find something positive to say.

    + Be **Interested**. Genuinely listen and respect each customer.

    + **Communicate** that you care. Let others know you value them.

    + Be **Encouraging**. Build up customers and co-workers.

## Personalize your service.

+ Use your first name to help you connect quickly.

+ Use Mr. or Mrs. and their last name to show respect.

+ Take a personal interest in customers.

# 4

## E — THE EXCEED KEY

*Surprising customers with unexpected, positive experiences will do more than anything else to create customer loyalty.*

—MARSHALL FIELD

E — THE THIRD KEY OF GREAT SERVICE represents our desire to **Exceed** customers' expectations. When guests go to Disney World, a Ritz Carlton hotel, a Nordstrom department store, or a fine restaurant, they're not looking for *average* anything. They expect to be *wowed* — to have their *socks knocked off!*

Regent Hotels are very nice hotels. Each hotel does something unusual to accommodate the needs of guests who stay more than once. Regent creates a "likes and dislikes" profile for every repeat guest. Every associate and manager tries to learn as much as possible about the likes and dislikes and the wants and needs of guests in order to create a unique experience for future stays as well as their present stay. Here are just a few of the special things Regent Hotels do for their guests:

- Roger prefers diet Pepsi. Even though Regent does not stock Pepsi products, every time Roger stays at a Regent Hotel, a diet Pepsi is in a bucket of ice in his room and a six-pack is sitting nearby.

- Marlene likes foam pillows. When she stays at a Regent Hotel, housekeeping replaces the regular pillows on her bed with her favorite type of foam pillows.

- Jenny loves tulips. She once happened to mention to a bellman that tulips "brightened her day." So every time Jenny stays at a Regent Hotel, a fresh bouquet of tulips greets her when she enters her room.

- In the hotel restaurant, the chef is automatically alerted to guest preferences, dietary needs, and favorite foods so that food can be prepared exactly as guests like it.

- Waiters make a note of guests' favorite beer, wine, and champagne and then anticipate guests' needs by offering their favorite beverage before being asked.

No wonder Regent Hotels receive some of the highest marks in guest satisfaction. In any business, exceeding customer expectations is one of the most powerful tools you can use to create satisfied, but also loyal customers.

Every customer who visits the finest resorts or does business with the best companies *expects* excellent service. Exceeding is simply listening to the customer and doing whatever it takes to be excellent. It doesn't take all that much additional effort, but *wowing* customers is a great way to exceed their expectations:

- At a fast food drive-through window, a 17-year-old employee noticed a customer whose car had stalled. He asked another co-worker to cover for him, went to his car, grabbed his jumper cables, and started her car. Then he went back in the kitchen and made her a fresh order of food at no additional cost.

- At a local drug store, a woman with a cast on her foot hobbled into the store using a cane. A stock clerk noticed her and grabbed a wheelchair from the back. The clerk then took the woman to every item on her list and even gave her some information about new skin care products. What drug store do you think will have this customer's loyalty?

The challenge of using the **Exceed** key is that you must first *understand* what customers expect *before* you can begin to exceed their expectations:

## Basic Service Expectations

+ A clean, professional-looking building with clean restrooms

+ Products that are neat, orderly, and easy to locate

+ Customer-friendly policies that make doing business easy

+ Employees who are nicely dressed and know their products

+ Employees who provide prompt, efficient service

+ Employees who can take care of sales and also make returns

+ Employees who like helping people and have good attitudes

+ Employees who are friendly and pleasant to work with

+ Employees who listen to customers and resolve problems

+ A company that genuinely cares about its customers

In life and at work, you usually get what you give. The things you give tend to come back to you, perhaps not so much in the manner in which they were given, but they do have a way of returning in some form or another. That's why we need to carefully watch what we say and do: our comments, attitudes, and actions will most certainly be reciprocated one day. *Remember:* Be careful what bridges you burn; you'll be surprised how many times you'll have to cross them again one day. The flip side is also true. If you go out of your way to help others, if you go the extra mile and do the unexpected, you'll be surprised at the difference it will make in you, your service, and in the way others perceive you.

Exceeding expectations includes excelling at communicating with your customers: listening, following through, keeping your word, and striving to get to know your customers so that you can best understand their needs. Keep them informed about what's happening and what to expect. One of the best communications tools I've found is the KISS principle: *Keep It Short and Simple.* Most of us think we're good communicators, but what we say and how other people *perceive* us can lead to two completely different expectations and outcomes. The more uncomplicated you keep your communication, the more effective your message will be. Here are ten ways to simplify communication:

1. Genuinely listen. Give your undivided attention.

2. Actively listen. Summarize and repeat information.

3.   Use good eye contact. Look others directly in the eye.

4.   Use a friendly tone and add personality to your voice.

5.   Speak and relate to others on their level, not yours.

6.   Don't assume things. You just might be incorrect.

7.   Ask questions and give feedback. Clarify information.

8.   Keep it simple and clear because simple is more effective.

9.   Explain with simple terms, without being condescending.

10.   Give specific steps to identify actions or results expected.

None of these are difficult by themselves, but if you apply *all ten ways* to simplify communication, you will become a more effective communicator than probably 80% of the people you meet. Words tend to be neutral. It's not the words you use so much as *how you say them*, your tone of voice, and *what you do*, your actions and expressions, that convey meaning to another person.

The purpose of all communication is to clarify understanding or initiate some form of action. If you don't understand what your customer or your co-worker expects, communication breaks down. Be the one who takes ownership of the process and ensures that communication is effective and clearly understood by all sides.

*What can you do to make a difference
in the lives of others?*

Exceeding expectations also includes having a *whatever it takes* mindset. Your role in service, and really in life, is to help other people win and to accomplish what they came to your business to do. When they win, you win! While at Disneyland, I spent a month with a group promoting the theme park all over Japan. I learned a term called "saving face." Saving face simply means, "I want to make you look good in the eyes of others, so I'll say whatever I need to say and do whatever I need to do to make you look good in the eyes of others." That's a very positive philosophy. What can you do to make customers look good? With every customer, silently ask this question: "How can I help this person succeed today?" See if it doesn't make a difference in you and in them.

The **Exceed** key requires a little more time and effort to execute than the other four keys of GREAT Service, but by applying two or three of the ideas from this chapter, the **Exceed** key can be achieved in thirty seconds or less.

# A. APPLY THE POWER OF ASKING

*When you ask questions, you demonstrate your interest in others.*

A number of years ago, a college received a multimillion-dollar donation from a woman who lived in a nearby town. The donor was a long-time friend of the president of a college in the donor's own community. Upon hearing of his friend's generous contribution, the president was perplexed and wondered: why would his friend choose to give money to a competing college instead of his? Finally, the president mustered enough courage to invite his friend to dinner. During dinner, he asked why she had chosen to donate to another college and not one in her own community. Her response was simple: "Because they asked and you didn't."

A biblical principle in James 4:2 states, "You do not have because you do not ask." The most effective way to determine what customers want is to ask them. The power of asking questions opens doors and reveals many opportunities: how you can help others; what it takes to please them; and to learn how satisfied they are with you and your service.

In his book *How to Win Customers for Life*, Michael LeBoeuf refers to the "Platinum Questions." While customers are shopping with you and *before* they leave, Dr. LeBoeuf says you should ask every customer two questions:

- How are we doing?
- How can we get better?

The best way to meet customers' needs and understand what they want is to simply ask them! Asking questions demonstrates your interest in the customer and his or her needs. Customers' answers provide you with opportunities to satisfy their needs and create long-term relationships. What better way to provide great service than by asking questions while you still have an opportunity to improve.

39. **Ask, "Is there anything else I can do for you?"**
    Your goal is to ensure you have done everything possible to meet their needs. Sometimes customers forget about an item they wanted. By asking if there is anything else you can do, you might trigger their memory, which will allow you to take care of their needs "on the

spot." The simple act of asking lets customers know that you are willing to do whatever they need done to ensure their satisfaction. It also encourages customers to ask lingering questions or express concerns they might still have before leaving. When you ask customers a question, use an *inquisitive* tone of voice. It indicates you're genuinely interested.

40. **Make results-oriented requests.** If you want a customer to change what they're doing, find a tactful way to make your request. Customers don't *have to* do anything. Most people resent being told what to do, but they appreciate having an opportunity to give their input. They just want to be given an option rather than being forced. Avoid making demands such as *I need you to …* or *you have to …* or *you can't … .* Demanding language is insulting to customers. On the other hand, politely asking, *Would you be able to …* or *I'm sorry for any inconvenience, but would you …* or *I would really appreciate it if …,* is much more tactful and the results will be far more favorable. That especially applies to your co-workers.

41. **Ask determining questions.** To determine a solution to a situation, there are two basic kinds of questions to ask customers: open-ended

and closed-ended. Open-ended questions are questions that *cannot* be answered with a one or two-word response. Open-ended questions allow a customer to describe the *who, what, where, when, how,* and *why* of a circumstance. Open-ended questions encourage a customer to describe a problem or situation from his or her perspective and based on his or her expectations. Asking *what happened* and *what were you expecting* helps customers give much better descriptions. Closed-ended questions allow you to find the right solution to a situation. Closed-ended questions usually need only a one or two-word response from the customer: "If we finish it by 3:00, would that work for you?" or "I can order it in blue or do you prefer red?" Open-ended questions help you *understand the problem* from the customer's perspective whereas closed-ended questions help you *determine the best solution.*

## B. BE EXCEPTIONAL

*It is the little things you do that differentiate you from your competition.*

Be ready. If you expect customers to inquire about something, be prepared with an answer. If there is a best-selling item, have it ready. Never say, *I don't know*. Instead say, *Let me find the answer for you*. When an employee says, *I don't know*, and does *nothing* further, it is the equivalent of saying, *I couldn't care less*. Every employee's job is to have the answers or, at the very least, to find them and then get back to the customer. *I don't know* is not an answer to anything.

42. **Anticipate their needs.** One of the best ways to exceed expectations is to anticipate customers' needs. At Disney World, the main parking area is called the Ticket and Transportation Center or TTC. The TTC parking lot is about a mile from the entrance to the Magic Kingdom. Guests are often so excited when they arrive that they forget to make a note of where their car is parked. It's not unusual to see a family walking down row after row after midnight looking for their car. So what does Disney do when this happens? If a guest knows the approximate time they parked their car, Disney can tell them *precisely* what row it is in. Also, Security patrols the parking lot at night looking for guests who are lost or who have locked their keys in their car or who need an extra gallon of gas. Disney anticipates these types of problems and is ready with solutions.

Security has unlocked thousands of car doors and provided a gallon of gas to many otherwise frantic guests at no cost, thereby preventing a negative end-of-the-day experience. *That's exceeding expectations!*

*If service is about the experience, then the experience is how you make the customer feel.*

**43.  Create a positive, memorable experience.** Service is often about *the experience.* Most customers don't look solely at price or quality, but at several other factors as well: are the employees knowledgeable; what is their attitude; and especially, do they treat me with courtesy and respect? If you want to be exceptional, do something unusual for the customer. Often it is the special things you do that set you apart from the competition. Special things — the personal touches — often create memorable experiences that can wow and delight customers. If a customer's family is with them, always include the family members in the service experience, especially younger children. Are there "little extras" you can do in your department that make the service fun for customers? Do you have a "give away" for the kids to make shopping more enjoyable? Maybe it's a balloon, a piece of candy, a free sample, a smiley face button, or an inspiring quote for the day. I sometimes take our border collie Taylor to the drive through window of my bank. The teller always comments about him and gives him two doggie treats as well. It's not much, yet it's a big deal to me — and Taylor. Look for ways to make the service experience memorable.

44. **Work at exceeding the expectations of others.** Never be satisfied with good or *getting by* — they tend to hold you back. Never settle for being good when you have the capability to be *great*. There is an expression that states, "The greatest enemy of excellence is good." Being *good enough* is creating an artificial ceiling that precludes you from excellence. If you want to achieve excellence, then you must raise the expectations you set for yourself. Don't let anyone hold you back. YOU ultimately determine how far you go on the job and in life — not your boss, not the customer, but you alone!

*Never promise customers more than you can deliver, but always deliver more than you promise.*

45. **Under promise, over deliver.** Don't promise or imply you can deliver a product or service at a specific time unless you can do it! If you

say, "I'll have it ready by 2:00 this afternoon" and it isn't ready until noon tomorrow, you have *failed* to keep your word. But if you say, "I'll have it by 9:00 tomorrow morning" and you have it by 4:00 p.m. today, you've *exceeded* their expectations. Customers have a tendency to take you at your word. When they find they can't depend on your word, you lose integrity, respect, and credibility. Always strive to give more and to exceed their expectations.

## C. GO THE EXTRA MILE

*The people who win in life are the ones who do the little things — who give the personal touch and go the extra mile.*

Many of us do what it takes to get by, but little else. I find that people who succeed at just about every aspect of life, work, and relationships are the people who are not content with being average. They are people who constantly strive to challenge and stretch themselves to be better than average — to be excellent.

46. **The extra mile differentiates you from the competition.** There's a great expression that says, "There's very little traffic on the extra

mile." That's because very few people are willing to go the extra mile or to do the extra things that make a difference. Going the extra mile is not all that difficult; yet few things differentiate you from others more than the extra mile. Here are a few examples of individuals who exceeded expectations. They went the extra mile:

+ A department store advertised a sale on a nice dress shirt. A customer had traveled 20 miles just to purchase one of the shirts, but the store had run out. Rather than giving a "rain check," the clerk asked the customer to wait for just a few minutes, saying he would be right back. The clerk then hurried to a competitor's store in the mall, purchased the same shirt at retail, returned, and sold the shirt to the customer at the sale price. End result: one very happy customer.

+ At a Country Inn and Suites in North Dakota, fifteen rooms had been reserved for several days in February for a large family reunion. When the family arrived, they found that the pool had to be closed for repairs. Management realized that not being able to swim would be a major disappointment for the kids. Rather than moving the reunion, Country Inn arranged to use the pool at a neighboring hotel and bought pizzas for the entire reunion party. End result: the family held their reunions at that Country Inn and Suites for the next 10 years. Not a bad investment.

+ At one of the Disney hotels, a housekeeper thought it would be fun to arrange plush Disney characters on the beds with a note welcoming the family back to their room after a busy day visiting one of the theme parks. The family loved it and couldn't wait to see what surprise awaited them the next day.

+ A group of friends took a buddy to a restaurant to celebrate his birthday. His friends arranged with the staff to have their buddy called to the lobby to take a bogus telephone call. When he returned to the dining area, the wait staff had encouraged everyone in the restaurant to sing "Happy Birthday." Then they all applauded. He returned to his seat, red faced, humbled, and honored.

+ When I lived in Orlando, my dentist was Tony Clements. Tony is the most memorable dentist I've ever had. He did something very unusual. Every time I had a cavity filled or had some other type of dental work done, not only did Tony do a great job, but he also called to check on me at 6:00 p.m. that same evening. Just about every time, I could set my watch by Tony's call! That's just one of the things that made Tony exceptional.

+ At Disney World, one of the shows was called "Dockside Jubilee." As part of one number, the performers left the stage to sing to members of the audience. One of the performers loved to sing to kids and during one performance he got down on one knee and sang to a little four-year-old girl for maybe 15 seconds. From her reaction, you would have thought he was Elvis! Her dad caught up with him after the show and told the singer what an impact it had on her and how much he appreciated the gesture. It was a little thing, but to her family it was a very big deal.

47. **Little things make the difference.** GREAT Service is also about doing the little things: remembering customers' names; listening and responding to them; including their families in conversation; offering them a cup of coffee; suggesting a sale or new item; asking what else you can do for them; and ensuring they are satisfied. In life as well as in service, it's not the

big things that make the difference. Usually it's the little things. Doing the little things make experiences memorable. Take a close look at your business. What are some little things you can do for your customers that will differentiate you from the competition?

48. **Add *Lagniappe* to your service.** Lagniappe (pronounced *lan-yap*) is a French Creole term used in the late 1800s in Louisiana. When a customer entered a merchant's store to purchase a pound of butter, the merchant would scoop out a pound, place it on the scale, and then reach back into the barrel, add another scoop and say "lagniappe," which means "I value you and am giving you a little extra to show I do." When you *lagniappe* a customer, you're saying, "How can I give you more than you expect?" In today's competitive climate, you have to give a little extra to stand out from the competition. Disney World taught me to differentiate myself from others by the little extras I gave to my customers. Some call it value-added service, but when you give a little extra, you reinforce the importance of customers and demonstrate how much you value their business. The great thing about *lagniappe* is that it can be as simple as a smile; or going out of your way to find

something a customer is looking for; or taking a customer to their destination rather than simply pointing or explaining; or offering a balloon to an upset child; or using a Donald Duck voice to distract a crying baby. Little extras make all the difference!

49. **Make service positive and fun.** One of the most effective attributes any employee can have is a sense of humor. Service doesn't always have to be serious, *so lighten up!* Many customers enjoy the interaction more when you make the service process fun. So when appropriate, loosen up and have fun. Working with difficult customers or challenging co-workers can be very stressful, but you can't keep things bottled up inside and still be effective. If you always take yourself or your work so seriously that you never have fun or enjoy yourself, you're like a "ticking time bomb." Employees who have no sense of humor are often dull, boring, and not much fun to be around. I guarantee: if you make the service experience fun in an appropriate way, work will be a much more enjoyable experience for everyone, especially you.

50. **Help others be successful.** If you want to change your perception of others, try this. The next time you work with a customer, especially

a difficult one, silently ask: *How can I help this person get what he wants?* Usually customers are so concerned about themselves and their families' needs that they don't think about you and your needs. Yet, if first and foremost you think in terms of your customers and what they want, you will change your perception of them. To do this, simply ask yourself:

+ How can I help this person?

+ What is it that he needs?

+ What can I do to help meet her wants and needs?

## Essential Ideas from the Exceed Key

Of the five keys of GREAT Service, using the **Exceed** key is the most time consuming. You cannot be excellent and be average, so exceeding expectations takes service to the level of excellence. It's true, you do get what you give and what you give is often returned to you. To be successful, you must have a *whatever it takes* mindset and go the extra mile to do the little things that help differentiate you from others.

## Apply the power of asking.

+ Ask, *Is there anything else I can do for you?* to satisfy them.

+ To get more favorable results, don't be demanding.

+ Use open-ended and closed-ended questions to resolve issues.

## Be exceptional.

+ Anticipate customer's needs and think ahead.

+ Create a positive experience. Make service fun and memorable.

+ Always strive to deliver more than you promise.

## Go the extra mile.

+ The extra mile differentiates you from others.

+ It is usually the little things that make the difference.

+ Add a little *lagniappe* to add value to your service.

# 5

## A — THE AFFIRM KEY

A — THE FOURTH KEY OF GREAT Service, is to **Affirm** every customer as well as your co-workers. Maybe you don't think of affirming customers and co-workers as part of service. You might even see this key as superficial or unnecessary, but I assure you that most people you encounter feel underappreciated. The purpose of the **Affirm** key is to make customers feel important. This chapter is dedicated to building people up and finding ways to demonstrate respect.

There is no such thing as a perfect company. Why? Because *people* run companies and *people are imperfect.* Everyone tends to become stressed out, make mistakes, or fall short at times. Disney World was a great place to work, but even Disney World could be stressful. Do you think it is easy being *The Happiest Place on Earth?* Many times it was, but sometimes keeping angry or impatient guests happy was very difficult. Yet, my responsibility was always to make every guest feel important, listened to, accepted, understood, and special. I'm certain that applies to your company and your customers as well.

I think many companies, and therefore employees, "miss the boat" when it comes to applying the **Affirm** key. They do a good job welcoming customers. They make certain they take good care of customers during the sales process, but after the sale they do very little to maintain a positive, ongoing relationship.

Several years ago, we decided to buy a brand new, top-of-the-line minivan. I have owned a number of cars in my life, but all of them had been used. So I did my research and found a dealership that promised great service. During the initial process, my salesman was great. He "bent over backwards" to get the sale. It seemed like he was willing to do anything for me. He called every few days to keep me posted on the delivery date and to see what else he could do. Six weeks later when the van finally arrived, my salesman made a very big deal about giving me the keys. But from that day forward, I felt abandoned by him *and* the dealership. There was no card or letter or telephone call to see if I was satisfied. When I had issues with the van or was dissatisfied with the service I'd received, I felt like I was on my own. When I called my salesman or stopped by the dealership, he made me feel like I was just another complaining customer.

I didn't expect my salesman to treat me like a king, but I did expect *some* type of follow up to see how we were doing and to see if I was a satisfied customer. When I stopped in the dealership for service, he could have invited me to his office for a cup of coffee or asked if I was pleased with their service department and the van. Those little things would have made me think he truly cared about me and not just about the sale. Maybe I'm unusual, but I don't think most customers appreciate the "bought and forgot" kind of service.

The **Affirm** key is really about showing customers and co-workers that you respect and appreciate them. Make your customers and co-workers feel that they are important. Executing the **Affirm** key requires only a few seconds of your time.

## A. VALIDATE EACH PERSON

*Express sincere appreciation
for every person you encounter.*

Everyone wants to feel significant. Everyone you encounter, including yourself, listens to the same radio station. The call letters are WII-FM, which means *What's In It For Me*. People tend to see things from their perspective, not yours. They are far more interested in themselves than they ever will be in you. That's not being selfish. That's just the way it is.

During Oprah Winfrey's *20th Anniversary Special*, something was said that I thought was quite profound: Oprah said that she has interviewed thousands of people over the past twenty years, from paupers to billionaires, and has found that all people have one thing in common — *they want to feel validated*. In a nutshell, I believe validation is the essence of a great customer service experience: to help each customer to feel that they are important and essential.

At a conference on *Improving Morale in the Workplace*, the facilitator made a statement: "If at any point in the conference today, you feel you need a little praise or feel you are not getting the attention you deserve at work, simply stand up and say, 'I need to be appreciated' and we'll stop and give you a standing ovation." No more than 10 minutes later, a young man stood up and said, "I need to feel appreciated!" So, the entire group stood up and gave him a standing ovation. About five minutes later, a middle-aged woman stood up, interrupted the speaker, and said, "I need to feel appreciated." That little scenario happened nearly twenty times during the four-hour conference, which shows that many people feel unimportant and underappreciated at work. Maybe it's because they don't feel appreciated anywhere else either.

**51.** **Validate everyone you meet.** *Validate* simply means to listen to others; to find positive attributes they have; and to look for ways to affirm them and build them up. No matter who a person is, there is an unspoken desire to feel significant. Everyone wants to feel that they are intelligent and that their opinion is correct. Never put someone down or belittle them, even if you're "just kidding." Even little insults can be detrimental to another person's self-esteem and self-worth. Sometimes, we have a tendency to be callous or insensitive to the needs and feelings of customers and co-workers. Put yourself in their shoes. *Remember:* Everyone you meet wants to be validated.

> *The deepest principle of human nature is the craving to be appreciated.*
> —WILLIAM JAMES

**52.** **Apply the MMFI principle.** Everyone you know is wearing a sign around their neck. The sign is invisible, but nevertheless it's there. For some people, the sign is small; for others, it's normal size; but for a few, it's enormous. The sign has four letters: MMFI, which means *Make Me Feel Important.* Your customers and your co-workers want to feel important. If you want to make a difference in others, look for ways to make everyone you encounter feel important and valued.

53. **Reward and reinforce excellence in your co-workers.** Reward your co-workers with praise every chance you get. Let them know when they do an excellent job. In today's economy, we need to support and affirm each other. According to an old adage, "The things that get rewarded get repeated." If you want to see excellence in your co-workers, compliment them. Don't just say *nice job*. Let them know exactly what they did and why it was exceptional. But never give false praise or be insincere; just provide genuine support and affirmation. I guarantee that your co-workers will appreciate it.

# B. INVEST IN OTHERS

*Demonstrate that people are important*
*— invest in their success.*

The best investment you can make is to improve you! By improving yourself, you will be better prepared to serve others. The next best investment you can make is in your co-workers. Investing in your co-workers is about teamwork and "making the dream" work. As I mentioned in the *Introduction*, the person who had the most impact on me didn't even work in my department. But we worked on numerous projects together, and he saw potential in me and challenged me to use my potential to the "max." He invested his time and resources in me to ensure my success and I am indebted to him.

You have co-workers who can receive tremendous benefits from your talents and abilities. But you'll never discover how you can help them until you get to know them: their dreams, their aspirations, any help they might need, and ways in which you can encourage and challenge them to be their best. Like any successful partnership, your relationship with your co-workers must be cultivated over time. Why not invite a co-worker to join you for lunch or break or for coffee? Spending time getting to know your team members builds trust and understanding. Investing in people means putting them first, not for what you can *gain* from them, but for what you can *give* to them. Helping others is truly at the heart of service!

54.  **Compliment your peers.** Giving praise is one of the best ways to affirm your peers and co-workers, as well as anyone else you come in contact with. In my training, I use a sheet that has some simple ideas to use when affirming others. It's called *50 Ways to Praise Others.* Here are just a few comments you can say to affirm others:

- I really appreciate your help with ...
- Wow, what a great job!
- Thank you for all the ...
- I really appreciate you for ...
- That was incredible! How did you ...
- You've made my day! Thank you.
- You really made the difference.
- We could not have done it without you.

Complimenting and praising your peers and co-workers doesn't take a whole lot of effort or words. Maybe it sounds trivial and insignificant, but your words might be the only thanks they have received in a long time. What better way to affirm your co-workers than to give a sincere, heart-felt compliment to someone who has done a great job or who just needs to hear *thank you* from someone they share the trenches with day after day.

55. **Challenge others to develop.** One of your responsibilities in life is to help those around you to grow. Everyone has untapped talent and abilities. Oftentimes you can see abilities in your co-workers that they cannot. Rather than being critical, look for their hidden potential. I challenge you to help each of your co-workers to grow personally: to be better equipped to face

customers; to be better prepared to work with each other; and to achieve their full potential. Help your co-workers to be the best they can be.

56. **Be an encourager.** Look for ways to "stretch" and motivate them. Often there is one person in every group that just about everyone wants to be around. This person has the *gift of encouragement* and builds other people up. Become known as a person who is always positive and encourages other people. I can't think of a greater compliment than "What a pleasure it is to work with her. She brings out the best in everyone." Work can be tough. Be the person who gives people hope and challenges others to be better, to go for that promotion, to develop their mind and body, and to exercise their skills and grow. Be the person who holds others accountable for losing weight, for getting off cigarettes, for kicking drugs or drinking, or to improve their relationships with others. Everyone needs mentors and coaches to help them do what they can't do on their own. Be an encourager who brings out the best in others!

# C. RECOVERY IS ESSENTIAL

*Recovery is critical if you want customers to
return and recommend you.*

Disney still makes mistakes — and so does every
other excellent company. The difference between
excellent and mediocre companies is often in how
well and how quickly they *recover* from their mistakes. Successful companies recognize that solving
problems of dissatisfied customers is frequently the
determining factor between saving and losing them.
Successful companies do whatever they can to immediately resolve customer issues.

I recently heard a story about a manager of a
casual dining restaurant. A customer had come in
and purchased a meal. She took the leftovers home
for her dog and put them in her refrigerator, but forgot about them for over a week. When she fed them
to her dog, the dog got sick. When she complained
to the manager of the restaurant, he listened, apologized, and then gave her a free meal. When asked
why he gave her a free meal when it was her fault
the dog got sick, the manager responded, "If I don't,
I may well lose a customer and I would much rather
'comp her' a $7 meal than risk losing her and all her
friends for life." That's a wise manager.

The most powerful advertising in the world is "word of mouth." People trust the advice of a friend or family member more than a slick $2 million ad during the Super Bowl. Word of mouth advertising doesn't cost you *anything*, yet it can cost you *everything*. Good or bad, people tell others about you and your service.

When there is a service recovery issue, you actually have two problems to fix: first is the problem itself and second is the frustration it has caused the customer. "Do the right thing" for customers. Ask yourself: *What is best for them?* Ask yourself: *How can I help them win?* First, fix the problem. Then go the extra mile to create a positive experience and a satisfied customer.

57. **Apply the ten-minute rule.** When you discover a service-related issue, *you own* the problem for the first ten minutes. Regardless of who caused the problem, you can either place blame or find a solution. The ten-minute rule has three steps:

   1. For the first ten minutes, do everything you can to resolve a customer's problem. It is far easier to resolve problems in the early stages before they have time to escalate.

   2. After ten minutes, turn the problem over to a teammate or a manager. Sometimes a wall

or a personality conflict develops between an employee and an upset customer. By turning the problem over to someone else, it might get resolved, whereas you were at an impasse. The important thing is to resolve the problem, period.

3. Follow up. Don't forget that you still own the problem. You are responsible for its solution.

58. **Use the LEARN System© of service recovery.** I have developed a simple system to help remember the important steps of service recovery. It's called LEARN: Listen, Empathize, Apologize, Resolve, and Normalize:

+ **Listen:** Let customers vent their frustration. Sometimes they're angry and all they want to do is to vent to get it off their chest. So be quiet and listen!

+ **Empathize:** Try to understand and relate to customers' concerns. Put yourself in their shoes. How would you feel? Would you feel you were being treated fairly?

+ **Apologize:** Be quick to apologize and say, *I'm sorry. I'm sorry* does not admit guilt. It simply means you're sorry for any inconvenience.

+ **Resolve:** Within reason, do whatever it takes to fix a problem. Your goal is to keep the customer by turning negative situations into positive experiences.

+ **Normalize:** The purpose of service recovery is to have customers return to either a neutral or positive position with you.

If a customer tells you about a service problem, take ownership to resolve the problem as quickly as possible. Whether you use the five LEARN steps or some other system, make resolving customer issues immediately a priority.

## Essential Ideas from the Affirm Key

**Affirm**, the fourth key of GREAT Service, is to demonstrate respect for others and to build them up. Every person has a need to feel important and significant. Many customers and co-workers rarely receive the appreciation or thanks they need. The key is to *help them succeed.* Ensure that your customers and co-workers feel important. Vital parts of the **Affirm** key are to recover from service problems as quickly as possible and to turn negative situations into positive experiences.

## Validate each person.

+ Remember WII-FM radio and think in terms of others.

+ Try MMFI in order to make *Make Me Feel Important*.

+ Reward and reinforce excellence in your co-workers.

## Invest in others.

+ Look for ways to compliment your peers.

+ Challenge and stretch others to reach their potential.

+ Be an encourager and bring out the best in other people.

## Recovery is essential.

+ Use LEARN to turn negative experiences into positive ones.

    + **Listen:** Let customers vent frustrations.

    + **Empathize:** Put yourself in the customer's shoes.

    + **Apologize:** Be quick to apologize or say *I'm sorry*.

    + **Resolve:** Take care of problems immediately.

# 6

## T — THE THANK KEY

T — THE FIFTH KEY OF GREAT Service, is the *icing on the cake*. Use the **Thank** key with every customer who comes to your department or business. Also use the **Thank** key with each of your co-workers whenever you have a chance. Just as using the **Greet** key creates a positive first impression with the customer, using the **Thank** key leaves a lasting one.

I recently heard a story about a new employee at K-Mart. It was her first day using a cash register and her trainer was standing right next to her assisting her. As she waited on her first customer, the trainer said, "Don't forget TYFSAK." Puzzled, the new cashier turned and asked, "What?" The trainer said, "TYFSAK. Don't forget to tell the customers 'TYFSAK!'" Still puzzled the new cashier turned to the customer and said, "TYFSAK." The customer, now confused as well, grabbed her bags and left. The trainer then said to her new cashier, "You weren't supposed to say 'TYFSAK,' you were supposed to tell her, 'Thank you for shopping at K-Mart!'"

I had the privilege of working for some excellent managers at Disney World. One who really stood out was Rich. He possessed excellent people skills and easily connected with frontline staff as well as his management peers. Rich was gifted at making people feel important. He always made sure he thanked each cast member in his department every chance he had. Rich kept a box of thank you cards in his desk. He had the habit of writing several notes a day to members of his team to express his gratitude.

One of the best things I learned from Rich was that every person I meet wants to feel appreciated and be thanked. So I created a little *thank you* reminder that I call TAG. It reminds me of the game you probably played as a kid. If you remember, the purpose of the game was to tag someone as quickly as possible so that they were "it," not you. The idea of the game was to get the attention off of you and on to someone else as quickly as possible. TAG simply means to give thanks, appreciation, and gratitude to other people. **Thank** them. Demonstrate your **Appreciation**. Express your **Gratitude**. In service, the goal is to get the focus off of employees and onto customers. In other words, "TAG, you're it!"

I once worked for a company where the morale in one department was terrible. A new manager was brought in to bolster employee morale and the image of the department. After observing the department and talking to many of his employees, he found that just about every one disliked their job and wanted to get out of the department. He couldn't get anyone to pick up shifts or work overtime or to transfer in from another department. The negative reputation had spread outside the company, so even newly hired employees refused to work in the department.

Out of sheer desperation, the new manager decided to try something that hadn't been tried before. Each day, during the last half hour of his shift, he went to every employee still on the job and personally thanked them for the job they were doing that day or had done that week. The first couple of weeks, his employees laughed and talked behind his back about his compliments. But after a few weeks, they began to appreciate them. Soon much of the backbiting and negative comments about the boss and about each other had ceased. They actually began to look forward to the daily support and appreciation they received from him.

In less than nine months, this department went from being the absolute worst in the company to being tied for best! When asked how he was able to turn his department around so dramatically, the manager replied, "I realized that the one missing ingredient was showing a little sincere appreciation for their hard work. I owe it all to one thing — every-day I simply thank each person for what they are already doing."

I once saw a plaque on a manager's wall that read: "Firings will continue until morale improves!" *I presume it was a joke.* This next statement is even more disconcerting because I've actually heard two different managers say it to their employees: "Your continued paycheck is the *only* thanks you need!" How would you like to work for either of those managers?

Many employees feel under-appreciated and taken for granted. They're seldom thanked by anyone for what they do day in and day out. Employees want to work with a manager who cares about them and respects them.

## A. THANK YOUR CUSTOMERS

*Make the effort to thank people every chance you have.*

The other day, I was on the Internet and wondered just how many theme parks are competing for our dollars. I discovered that there are over fifty theme parks across the country! Now, some of these parks aren't very big, and some are carnivals or amusement parks, but they still call themselves theme parks. Each one of them competes for our entertainment dollars.

Not only are theme parks competing for our dollars, but so are movie theaters, music concerts, grocery stores, restaurants, and hotels. Just about everyone is competing for the same discretionary dollars. Your company is in competition with those companies and others as well. Customers are carefully deciding where to spend their hard-earned money. Especially in a tight economy, employees must go out of their way to provide great service. One of the best ways to differentiate yourself from others is to thank customers and show your appreciation for their loyalty. Thanking customers leaves a powerful lasting impression and it only requires a few seconds.

59.  **Thank customers for choosing to do business with you.** Without customers, you're out of business. They have a choice. They don't have to do business with anyone. With the onset of the Internet, they can easily take their business to your competitors. If it weren't for customers, no one in your company would have a job. When customers come through your doors, they have made a conscious choice to do business with your company. At the very least, they deserve your thanks. Thank your customers for coming

in and for placing their trust in you, your products, and services. When customers sense you genuinely appreciate them, they are more likely to return and tell their friends. They make it possible for you to have a job and for your company to grow and make a profit.

*The ultimate purpose of a business is to gain and retain customers.*

60.   **Thank customers for their patience.** When you're busy or there is a problem, thank your customers for their patience. Some customers become demanding and even belligerent when they don't get the service they want or if the service is taking longer than expected. A simple *I'm sorry for the delay* can do wonders to ease the tension. Here's another way to help diffuse frustration. If you know a problem is about to occur, simply say, *I want to thank you in advance for your patience with …. We are doing everything we can to resolve it as quickly as possible.* That statement has a way of taking the wind out of their frustration. Most customers are very forgiving if you ask for their patience or prepare them in advance.

61. **Thank customers when they complain.** Even though it sounds strange, a complaint can be a gift. When a customer complains, he or she is obviously upset about something that has not gone the way they expected. Sometimes a customer's complaint is the only way to make you aware of a problem. But many customers don't do their complaining with their mouths; they do it with their feet. They leave, tell their friends, and never come back. Thanking a customer for a complaint not only gives you a chance to resolve a problem or concern, but it also lets the customer know that you appreciate having the opportunity to make it right. When a customer gives you input about your services or your products, whether it's a complaint or a positive comment, thank them for the opportunity to improve and to reinforce what you do for them.

62. **Thank customers by inviting them back.** When customers leave, tell them how much you appreciate their business. Let them know with a simple, *Thanks. Please come again* or *I look forward to seeing you again* or *I hope you'll return soon.* A great way to be thanked by a customer is for him or her to say, *I'll be back.* From a customer, there are few higher compliments a business can receive. When a customer says *I'll*

*be back,* she is actually saying, *I'm pleased with you and your service and I'll come here again.*

## B. FIND OTHER WAYS TO SAY THANK YOU

*Look for special ways to thank people everyday.*

The movie, "Facing the Giants," is about a struggling football coach who started off the season losing his first three games. Some parents and the school board even considered firing the coach early in the season. But the coach decided to challenge each member of his football team to "give their best" regardless of the outcome. His challenge changed the football team from losers to winners, and it also changed the character of each young man.

After one of the fathers saw what a dramatic difference the coach had made in his son, he said *thank you* in a very unique way. The coach owned a broken down old "bomb" for a car. After practice one day he went to the parking lot, but found that his car was not there. The only vehicle left in the parking lot was a brand new red pickup truck. On the truck was a note thanking the coach for the difference he had made in the man's son as well as the entire team. Now this was a movie and most of us can't afford to give away pickup trucks, but we can do things that say *thank you* to let others know how much they are appreciated.

63. **Do random acts of kindness.** A great way to thank others is by doing random acts of kindness. If you want to do something that will make you feel really good about yourself, try doing something for someone else, without their knowing about it and without expecting any kind of payback. You will be amazed how a random act of kindness will positively impact others and even give them a desire to do the same for other people. Here are a couple of great questions to ask yourself:

   • What can *I* do for someone else that will make their day?

   • How can *I* do an act of kindness for someone without their knowing about it?

64. **Show gratitude.** Having an attitude of gratitude is powerful. When I performed at Disney World, a fellow cast member once told me that I had done a great job singing a solo. But I knew I hadn't done my best and I told him so. He thought for a moment and then proceeded to chastise me for insulting him! You see, from his perspective, I *had* done an excellent job and for me to discount his compliment was a slap in the face. He taught me a valuable lesson:

the compliment was about *his* opinion, not *mine*; regardless of how I felt, I should have been grateful. Now, I make every effort to sincerely thank anyone who compliments me because I recognize the compliment is genuine. Gratitude is being appreciative of what others say or do for you. Gratitude is not false pride, but rather demonstrating respect and sincere appreciation.

65. **Say *thank you.*** Here are ten ways to say thank you without using the words:

    1. Tell someone you noticed something special they did.

    2. Give someone an opportunity to do something they like to do.

    3. Listen to a request and then act on it.

    4. Offer to help someone without being asked.

    5. Do something special for someone without their knowledge.

    6. Say, *That was a very nice thing to do.*

    7. Say, *I really appreciate your patience.*

    8. Say, *You'll never know what that means to me.*

    9. Say, *Here's what I'd like to do for you* and then do it.

    10. Say, *I really appreciate your help with that customer.*

# C. THANK YOUR CO-WORKERS AND YOUR BOSS

*Let your co-workers know that they are just as important as your customers.*

Your co-workers are your support team. Many of them rarely are thanked, yet they deserve the same gratitude and appreciation as your customers. Here are some ways to express your gratitude:

+ Send a handwritten note of appreciation to a co-worker (a telephone call or an email are the second and third best things to do).

+ Give a co-worker a gift certificate for a movie or her favorite restaurant.

+ Tell your boss about something special a co-worker did. Ask your boss if you may place a note about it in the co-worker's file.

+ Invite a co-worker to lunch. Tell him why you appreciate him. *Be sure to pick up the tab!*

+ Take a picture of a co-worker or your boss doing something out of the ordinary and post it on the employee bulletin board.

+ Write an accolade for your company's newsletter about something exceptional a co-worker did for someone else.

If you have ever been in a leadership position you know what a thankless job it can be. At a company where I once worked, there were some problems. One of the frontline employees chided, "That's why management gets paid the big bucks!" When I talked to their manager, I asked him, "How much more do you make than your frontline employees?" He said, "Forty bucks a week." People and employee issues are very taxing. An extra few dollars don't make problems any easier. Where does a manager go to vent when he or she is stressed to the "max" and doesn't know the right answer? My advice: give your manager a little slack:

- Let your manager know you support him and then look for opportunities to encourage him.

- Send your boss a personal note or an email once a month to encourage her.

- Send him an article on a subject he has been struggling with.

Most managers really appreciate encouragement and support from their staff. Do the same for your co-workers as well.

66. **Thank co-workers daily for their help.** One of the best ways to improve service is to improve your relationships with co-workers. Thank them for their help, support, and cooperation.

When co-workers do a good job, tell them you noticed what they did. When they need assistance, offer your help *before* they ask. When you finish a task or go through a tough time together, sincerely thank your co-workers. If it was a big deal, buy pizzas for break or throw a party to show your appreciation. Make it a special event. The more your co-workers feel appreciated, the more willing they will be to assist you the next time you need their support. Making the team look good benefits everyone.

*The deepest urge of human nature
is the desire to be important.*
—JOHN DEWEY

67. **Let co-workers know they are valued and valuable.** Recently, I heard a story about Ben Franklin. Ben had an enemy he just couldn't get along with. He tried everything he could to befriend this man. One day Ben saw the man reading a book, so he inquired about the book. Then Ben asked if he could borrow the book saying, "It sounds quite interesting." The man was so flattered that he loaned Franklin the book and later they discussed it at length. From that point on they became lifelong friends. It may sound strange, but one of the best ways

to express the value of another person is to ask them to do something for you or to help you. Call it human nature, but most people feel honored to be asked for their help, but only when the request is sincere and not imposing or manipulative. Simply stated, when you ask others for help, you are actually demonstrating your appreciation of them. Every person wants to feel valued, significant, and important. Show that you value customers by encouraging, supporting, thanking, and expressing your appreciation.

68. **Thank your boss for his or her support.** It surprises me when disgruntled employees say their boss is a machine or a robot and that he or she has no feelings. Once a vice president who was responsible for thousands of employees confided in me, "Why don't people like me?" Even top management faces many of the same issues you do. I've been on both sides. It isn't easy to be a manager who has to make tough decisions. Most managers would love to be in a workplace where everything goes smoothly and without a hitch and to have employees who love their jobs and appreciate their managers. If you find that company, let me know because I don't think it exists. Being a manager can be a

very lonely job. The job becomes all the more difficult when employees cut him down behind his back. I wish some employees could sit in on conversations I've had with managers who are frustrated because the budget is tight or because an employee has slipped from being an excellent worker to being apathetic. Employees need to see how hard it is to terminate an employee who violates company policy by stealing just one Coke without paying for it. Not only does the employee lose his job and his income, but he will also lose benefits for his family. Your boss has a difficult job and without your support, respect, and encouragement, his or her job becomes much more difficult. Instead of cutting down or making fun of your boss, do things that will have a positive impact:

+ Let your boss know when you think he has done a great job.

+ Tell your boss what you appreciate about her leadership qualities.

+ Stand up for your boss even when others unfairly cut him down.

+ Encourage your boss when she has to make a difficult decision.

**69.** **Write notes of thanks.** With the advent of email, much of the personal touch associated with handwritten notes has been lost. A great way to thank and encourage others is with handwritten notes. It's better than a telephone call and more personal than email. People really appreciate receiving thank you cards. Many employees read the card over and over. If you want to set yourself apart, set a goal to write at least three notes each week. You'll be surprised at the positive impact thank you cards can have on others and you'll make their day.

## Essential Ideas from the Thank Key

The **Thank** key is the icing on the cake of GREAT Service. Using the **Thank** key is a great way to show customers you appreciate them. It doesn't require much time, but it leaves them with a positive, lasting impression. Thanking customers and your co-workers is a simple gesture of respect and courtesy and it demonstrates their importance to you. Whether they buy something or not, express appreciation to every customer as they leave. *Remember TAG: Thank* them, show your *appreciation*, and express your *gratitude.*

## Thank your customers.

- Thank them for choosing to do business with you.

- Thank them for the complaints that help you improve.

- Thank them before and after for their patience with you.

## Find other ways to say thank you.

- Practice random acts of kindness for others.

- Express your gratitude and appreciation of others.

- Find unique ways to thank others for their assistance.

## Thank your co-workers and your boss.

- Thank your co-workers for their help and support.

- Let your boss know you appreciate and respect her.

- Make a habit of writing three thank you notes a week.

# 7

## THE LIKEABILITY FACTOR

THIS FINAL CHAPTER is actually an extension of Chapter 1, *Attitude Makes the Difference*. Yes, *attitude* is an essential component in service and in people relations too, but it's the *likeability factor* that makes a service experience enjoyable. Yet all too often likeability is missing in service. Employees who like people and enjoy helping customers tend to stand out from their peers and receive many more positive letters and comments. But some employees dislike working with customers and seem to resent the very idea of helping them. They stand out as well — they receive the bulk of complaints from customers and their co-workers.

Employees who possess the likeability factor tend to attract others. Customers enjoy being around them. Co-workers appreciate having an opportunity to work with them. But employees who lack the likeability factor tend to repel customers and co-workers. Sometimes they frustrate and even infuriate customers.

To get ahead in your relationships with others, look at the likeability skills you possess. Implement the basic human relationship skills you've learned over the years — the qualities that attract people rather than "turning them off." Cultivate being friendly and smiling; being courteous and respectful; listening more than you talk; putting other's wants before your own; complimenting, encouraging, and affirming others; expressing interest in others; and being kind and considerate instead of cold and abrasive. These are just a few qualities of likeability that make you *a more enjoyable person to be around.*

The people you spend the most time with will likely determine the kind of person you are. Have you ever heard the expression, "Misery loves company?" Negative people like to be with other negative people. When you associate with negative people, you tend to become negative as well. Yet people who associate with positive, enthusiastic, supportive people tend to become more positive and enthusiastic as a result.

Just like attitude and likeability, friendliness is essential in GREAT Service. The Magic Kingdom is one of my favorite places to observe friendliness, not only to see what friendly *looks* like, but more importantly to see how and why it works so well. You see, friendliness is also an attitude. Several months ago I saw a report on TV that stated: "Rudeness is at an all time high." When I shop in cities around the country, I am often disappointed by some of the attitudes I see. I don't see a lot of smiles or happy faces and I don't see many employees going out of their way to be friendly or helpful. As a matter of fact, I see a lot of apathy — companies that provide impersonal service and employees who seem to be going through the motions.

The ultimate factor in service is that you must first and foremost care about people. The caring must be genuine. You can only fake it for so long before the real you will come through. How many times have you watched a TV or movie star who seemed to be very personable, caring, and friendly on camera, but when you or a friend met this star in person, they were arrogant, condescending, and disingenuous? Which one was the *real person*: the persona on the screen or the individual you met in person? I assure you that one was acting and the other was real.

## A. BE FRIENDLY

*Life is like a mirror. You get what you give.*

It's true. You do get what you give. Isn't it funny when employees are negative, critical, and insensitive and then complain that work isn't fun and no one is friendly or gets along? I wonder if they ever think that

115

*they* might be the problem. Your company or department will be as nice, caring, and friendly as *you* make it — nothing more, nothing less. You have the power to change yourself, which is the beginning of improving your department and your company. **Remember:** If you want your job to be fun, or your co-workers to be a little nicer to deal with, it all starts with you.

Not everyone is good at helping customers and resolving complaints, but many are. It just comes naturally to them. They make taking care of customers a positive experience for everyone and seem to really enjoy helping other people. Then there are those who feel trapped in a job they don't like or aren't suited for and they're going nowhere. If you don't enjoy coming into work everyday, if you don't like helping customers find solutions, or if you are easily frustrated by customers, you probably are in the wrong job. If you're not content or happy in your job, leave! Life is too short to be in a job you don't enjoy.

I am a singer so I like to use this analogy: "Too many people finish their lives with the song still in them." You see, I believe each person has a *song*, a purpose they were designed to do. Your primary responsibility in life is to find out what that purpose is and then do it! I call it "finding your fit." *Content people are more enjoyable to be around.*

70. **The #1 attribute that will improve your business.** If I owned a service business and wanted to improve my business, the company's image, the employees, and customers' perceptions of my company, I would do my best to instill one attribute into every employee and manager in the company. That attribute would improve attitudes, teamwork, communication, respect, cooperation, and customer satisfaction. It would make work more fun and reduce stress, negativity, rumors, and much of the back biting. What would this *miraculous* attribute be? *Friendliness.* Here's why. When you are genuinely friendly, you come across as more competent, confident, and interested. You project that you like your job, that you care about other people, and that you're a good communicator. Some employees say, "We're professional. We don't need to be friendly!" That's arrogance! I'm not downplaying the importance of competence and knowledge, but imagine if every person in your company were friendly and worked at getting along well with each other. Would it not improve morale? Would it not improve attitudes? Would it not improve teamwork, respect, cooperation, and customer satisfaction and make work more enjoyable? Competence, a good attitude, and

knowledge are all important, but if I could instill just one attribute, more than any other, I would want you to be friendly and work at getting along with others because it affects and impacts virtually everything you do. *Friendly people are more enjoyable to be around.*

71. **Nice works.** Just because people are nice does not imply they are weak. People who are nice seem to naturally get along better with others. They tend to think in terms of other people and what they can do for them. Nice people make the world a better place to work and live. They are team players and everyone wants to work with them. Being rude, insensitive, and condescending is insulting and offensive — usually customers never want to do business again with people who act like that. In short, it's better to be nice and easy to get along with than to be a jerk. *Nice people are more enjoyable to be around.*

72. **Apply the *I like you* principle.** You treat people as you see them. The Director of Nurses at a hospital told me the following story. She had called Cathy, one of her nurses, into her office one day. The director said, "Cathy, when you make your rounds today, I'd like for you to do something for me. Before you enter a patient's

room, say to yourself, *I like you.* While you're working with the patient, say to yourself, *I like you.* Cathy responded, "That's silly, why?" The director said, "Please, as a favor to me, just do it." About six hours later, Cathy ran into her director and said, "You set me up!" The director said, "No, I didn't." Cathy responded, "Then why were all my patients so nice and friendly today?" The director said, "Cathy, you're a good nurse, but sometimes you're inconsistent. You tend to let petty little things affect your day and you take your bad mood into a patient's room. But, today you told yourself *I like you* before you even entered the patient's room and you projected to each patient that you genuinely liked them. They reciprocated and liked you back." Surprised, Cathy asked, "Would it work like that all the time?" "I'll bet it would," replied the director. Try using the *I like you* principle when you work with a customer or a hostile co-worker. You too will be surprised how effectively it can work for you. *Likeable people are more enjoyable to be around.*

73. **Think in terms of the other person.** Remember *What's In It For Me*, the WII-FM radio station that everyone listens to? Before employees even enter my training class, they probably have

already said to themselves, "Yeah, if I do this the company benefits, but what do I get out of it?" Understanding that, I provide "take aways" that apply to them as individuals. These ideas include tools, motivation, challenges, and tips to enrich their lives that they can use personally as well as professionally. Customers, co-workers, and just about everyone else you encounter is asking, *What's in it for me?* So think in terms of the other person: how can I help her? What does he need? **Remember:** Put others first. *Thoughtful people are more enjoyable to be around.*

## B. BE COURTEOUS

*The foundation of respect
begins with common courtesy.*

GREAT Service is about respecting others. I don't think it's possible to demonstrate respect for another person without using basic, common courtesies. And yet, common courtesies are no longer *common*. Treating people with civility and showing respect used to be commonplace, but now the courtesies we once took for granted are often nonexistent. The key to being courteous is to be sincere; otherwise you come across as disingenuous. Being curt, rude, or disrespectful to a customer or even your co-workers alienates them.

You show respect and acknowledge the value of others when you use common courtesies. When you view your time and personal interests as being more important than those of another, you devalue that person and can come across as a cold person. A cold person treats others as though they were insignificant. Respect is a two-way street. If you don't demonstrate respect for me, then don't expect me to respect you. *Respectful people are more enjoyable to be around.*

74. **Common courtesies are paramount!** If excellent service is your goal, then common courtesy is essential! Always say *please.* When you ask someone to do anything, saying *please* makes the difference between them feeling forced to do it or being requested to do it. *Thank you* and *you're welcome* are the flip sides of saying *please.* They show your appreciation. When you say *please,* accompany the action with *thank you* when it is completed. When someone says *thank you,* respond with *my pleasure.* In most cases, saying *my pleasure* is much more effective than saying *no problem.* For the purposes of this book, I have identified courtesies into two categories, *What to Say* and *What to Do:*

### What to Say

Please, thank you, and you're welcome

I'm sorry or excuse me

May I help you?

My pleasure (avoid saying *No problem*)

I'll find out or I'll be glad to (never say
   *I don't know*)

Mr. or Mrs. and their surname

Sir and ma'am (never say *Hey you!*)

Is there anything else I can do for you?

I appreciate your patience.

Thank you. Please come again.

### What to Do

Smile and make direct eye contact.

Genuinely listen and give your full attention.

Greet customers with a friendly tone of voice.

Use energy and enthusiasm.

Pay customers a compliment.

Be tactful and considerate.

Never argue or yell at a customer.

Don't be rude, insensitive, or indifferent.

Have integrity by keeping your word.

Follow up to ensure customer satisfaction.

Open the door or offer your assistance.

Avoid condescension or sarcasm.

Have a positive attitude and approach.

Take people to their destination.

Understand the importance and benefits of using common courtesies in your work and relationships. Make them an essential part of your daily routine. *Common courtesies make you more enjoyable to be around.*

## C. GET ALONG

*You can win more friends in two months*
*by becoming really interested in people than*
*you can in two years by trying to get*
*other people interested in you.*
—DALE CARNEGIE

According to an old adage: "You can catch more flies with honey than you can with vinegar." There is a lot of truth to that statement. How much cooperation do you get when you yell at someone, insult them, or cut them down? *Usually very little.* On the flip side, are co-workers and customers more likely to help or cooperate with you if you are complimentary and supportive of them or genuinely offer to help them?

*Absolutely!* The bottom line is this: you *must* get along with others if you want to succeed!

No matter how good your skills are, what kind of attitude you possess, or how well you can recite the ideas in this book, if you don't have or develop qualities that draw others to you, you will not be successful in any service-related career. No matter how many degrees or titles you have, if you do not have a cooperative spirit, a pleasant demeanor, and a likeable personality, co-workers will not want to work with you and customers will not want to do business with you or your company for long. And there are benefits:

+ Getting along creates a positive atmosphere.

+ Getting along enables you to accomplish more.

+ Getting along gains support from your co-workers.

+ Getting along makes people desire to be around you.

+ Getting along, makes you more positive and pleasant.

> *People who get along with others*
> *are more enjoyable to be around.*

75. **Why some employees get fired.** One of the primary reasons an employee is fired is not

because he lacks qualifications or she is unable to do the job or because he is tardy too often. Often it's because he or she *cannot get along* with other people: customers, their co-workers, or their boss. More so than knowledge and technical skills, your attitude, your people skills, and your ability to get along with other people determine how far you go in life and at work. If you can't work well with co-workers, you are actually sabotaging your success. Focus on areas you have in common with your co-workers rather than what divides you. Look for things that you agree on rather than the issues that cause conflict. When you support, respect, and encourage your co-workers, they will usually return the favor. *Supportive people are more enjoyable to be around.*

*Any fool can criticize, condemn,*
*and complain ... and most fools do.*
—DALE CARNEGIE

76. **Be tactful.** Respond to others with tact and sensitivity. Although it's very tempting to be sarcastic and cynical when someone is condescending toward you, always consider how your response will sound and how it might impact the other person *before* you say it. You

are accountable for every word that comes out of your mouth. Ask yourself, "Will my words build him up or tear him down?" If your words are destructive, do you really need to say them? Sometimes the best thing you can do is to keep your comments to yourself. My wife Lorrie is probably the most tactful person I know. She constantly looks for the good in others. Even if I make a comment about someone on TV, she always has a possible reason for their plight — maybe they've had a rough life or they're down on their luck. She always seems to take the side of the underdog, but her positive view of others challenges *me* to look for the best in people. Some individuals are just the opposite — they're blunt and direct. They don't seem to care if they insult other people or say hurtful things. Most people appreciate individuals who can make them feel good — especially when they've been criticized by others. Tactfulness is an important component of likeability. Tactful individuals tell other people the truth, but they also consider the other person's feelings and the effect their words may have. *Tactful people are more enjoyable to be around.*

**One final idea.** Sometimes you have to stretch yourself and get outside your comfort zone.

Sometimes you have to be a pioneer or a maverick; or take chances; or be different from everyone else to forge ahead. If you want to excel, never listen to the advice of negative people.

77. **Never be afraid to fail.** Throughout history, at some time in their lives, most successful people have been mocked or called failures. If you follow the advice of the critics and cynics you encounter, you will never accomplish anything. Here are just a few examples:

   + **Thomas Edison** was repeatedly told by his own father as a boy that he was stupid. Even Edison's teachers told him he would fail.

   + **Walt Disney** was fired from his first newspaper job after being told he had little talent as an artist.

   + **Colonel Harlan Sanders** was thought to be a colossal failure throughout his life. He used his first Social Security check to open a restaurant which he called Kentucky Fried Chicken.

   + **Clint Eastwood** was fired in 1959 by Universal Studios because management thought his Adam's apple was too big and no one would want to look at him.

- **Cesar Ritz**, founder of Ritz Carlton Hotels, was fired from his first hotel job by a boss who told him he had no flair for the hospitality industry.

- **Elvis Presley** was fired in 1954 from "The Grand Ole Opry" after a manager told him, "You ain't going nowhere, son. You should go back to truck driving."

- **The Beatles** were turned down by Decca Records in 1962 with the comment: "We don't like your sound. Guitar groups are on the way out."

As Zig Ziglar says, "You were designed for success. You were endowed with the seeds of greatness." Never let anyone deter you from greatness — from being what you were designed to be and do.

## Essential Ideas from the Likeability Factor

Having a good *attitude* is essential to providing GREAT Service, but it's *likeability* that makes the service experience *enjoyable*. Work at smiling and being friendly, courteous, and respectful and at listening more than you speak. You express interest in others when you put them first. Compliment, encourage, and affirm others. These are just a few qualities of likeability that impact *your* bottom line.

## Be friendly.

- The #1 attribute that will improve you is being friendly!
- Apply the *I like you* principle. Project likeability to others.
- Think in terms of other persons' wants, needs, and desires.

## Be courteous.

- Use common courtesies to demonstrate importance.
- Use *please, thank you,* and *you're welcome* everyday.
- Be considerate of *what you say* and *do* to others.

## Get along.

- Cooperation and teamwork are keys to success.
- Some employees who *can't get along* get fired.
- Be a tactful person and avoid destructive comments.

If you're not a people person or you don't enjoy helping others, then service is the wrong industry for you. Unless you enjoy working with people, you'll never be happy or fulfilled in any job that serves the public. If this is a description of you, here is my suggestion. Set goals to improve yourself. Determine where you want to go in your career. Get on the Internet or go to your local library and find books that focus on the career you want and on improving your people skills. If some of these books are not in your local library, you can go to the library reference desk and request these books through the Inter Library Loan System. The ILLS finds books on any subject in any library in the United States and ships them to your local library for free. Using your library and the ILLS, you can improve yourself and your career skills while still in your current position.

# CONCLUDING

# THOUGHTS

**W**ALT DISNEY WORLD was a tremendous experience for me, not only for what it gave me, but for what it has enabled me to give to others. Dennis Snow, a friend of mine, who also worked at Disney World, told a story about a friend who was teaching a seminar. At the seminar, one of the managers posed an interesting question: "What if I provide all the training and development that you suggest and it enables my employees to become successful and they leave? Then what?" His friend thought for a moment and responded, "What if you don't provide the training to help them succeed and they stay?" The manager thought for a moment and responded, "I hadn't thought about it that way."

Your job, whether you're a frontline employee, a manager, or the owner of the corporation, is to help other people become successful. Your ultimate job is to help each person you encounter to win. As Zig Ziglar says, "When you help enough other people win, you win!"

I leave you with words from Charles Swindoll, my favorite author and speaker. His words epitomize the importance of attitude in our lives and work.

## Attitude

*The longer I live, the more I realize the impact*
*of attitude on life.*
*Attitude to me is more important than facts.*

*It is more important than the past, than education,*
*than money, than circumstances, than failures,*
*than successes, than what other people think or say or do.*

*It is more important than appearance, giftedness, or skill.*
*It will make or break a company.*
*It will cause a church to soar or sink.*

*It will be the difference in a happy home*
*or a home of horror.*

*The remarkable thing is you have a choice every day*
*regarding the attitude you will embrace for that day.*

*We cannot change our past ... we cannot change*
*the fact that people will act a certain way.*

*We cannot change the inevitable.*

*The only thing we can do is play on the one string we have,*
*and that is our attitude.*

*I am convinced that life is 10% what happens to me*
*and 90% how I react to it.*
*And so it is with you.*

—Charles Swindoll

# ENDNOTES

Roger Ailes and Jon Kraushar (Collaborator). *You Are the Message*. New York: Random House/ Broadway Business; August 1989.

Dale Carnegie. *How to Win Friends and Influence People*. New York: Simon and Schuster; 1937.

Michael LeBoeuf. *How to Win Customers and Keep Them for Life*. New York: Penguin Group/ Berkley Trade; August 2000.

Albert Mehrabian. *Silent Messages: Implicit Communication of Emotions and Attitudes*. Belmont, CA: Wadsworth Publishing; June 1980.

Carl Sewell. *Customers for Life*. New York: Doubleday Business; September 1990.

Chuck Swindoll. *Strengthening Your Grip: Essentials in an Aimless World*. New York: Bantam Books; October 1986.